Mad Dogs And Queer Tattoos

Tattooing the San Francisco Queer Revolution

Robert E. Roberts

Mad Dogs And Queer Tattoos

Tattooing the San Francisco Queer Revolution

by Robert E. Roberts

Fair Page Media LLC
Springfield, PA

ISBN: 978-0-9989098-1-3

To all the people who came through the shop door and
allowed me put ink to their skin…

To the life-friends who loved me for what I am…

And to the memory of Timothy James Mounts

TABLE OF CONTENTS

Acknowledgments

Nice Guy Pauly (Paul Ranger), who kept nagging me to write my stories, and Wyatt Johnson, who seconded the motion.

Gene Rigler, friend and confidant who nursed me through this project and whose feedback is always thoughtfully targeted.

My late husband, Ed Swenson, who thought I was a nutcase but encouraged me all through the process.

"Bonsai Pete" Vafiades, friend, bartender, and plantsman extraordinaire, who helped me with details about the history of the Lone Star Saloon.

Christopher Harrity at *The Advocate*, who generously helped with research.

Rick Storer at the Leather Archives and Museum in Chicago, who helped me track down *Drummer* magazine articles.

Jack Fritscher, PhD, and C.W. (Chuck) Eldridge, whose generous and insightful testimonials are on the back of this book.

INTRODUCTION

"There is the truth of history, and there is the truth of what a person remembers."

- *Rebecca Wells*, Divine Secrets of the Ya-Ya Sisterhood

To be a professional tattooer is a pretty odd occupation, requiring a person to be part artist, part medic, part psychiatrist, and part *raconteur*. As a profession, tattooing is still associated in many people's minds with unsavory subcultural connotations, while for many others that's part of its appeal. To a large segment of the population, a tattooer isn't someone you want to know, much less invite to dinner, and seems to be only a little higher on the food chain than a door-to-door salesman of do-it-yourself knee-surgery kits. To the religious conservative "we'll stone you if you don't bow to our god" politicos, a tattooer is often viewed as a pernicious purveyor of sin on skin.

The tattoo world was, and still is, a predominantly straight, heterosexual environment. Even now, in the second decade of the 21st century, virtually all tattoo periodicals are targeted to a straight male audience, sporting lurid, curvaceous tattooed pinup types on every magazine cover, in their advertising and on their web sites. In more recent years, some tattoo magazines have stood up for gay rights in their articles, including support for marriage equality (*Inked* magazine, for one). In all fairness, it is neither the business nor the purpose of these publications to promote aspects of gay awareness. Instead of relying on the occasional magazine article, it is incumbent on us within the gay community to tell our stories and document our existence.

For me, the concepts of "gay" and "tattoo" are intertwined, forming part of my world view. For more than twenty years (1986 to 2007), I had the unique opportunity to work almost entirely within San Francisco's gay community. I worked alone — I didn't work in a walk-in shop, I advertised in only a couple of gay publications, and only occasionally did I have a heterosexual customer.

Gay tattooing *is* different. To begin to understand that difference, I have included a good deal of gay history that was happening around me at the time. This book, then, is as much about being a gay man as it is about tattooing.

There have been other notable gay tattooers in both the U.S. and abroad, but most of their day-to-day artistic output had to fall within a larger straight context. Business is business, after all. Identifiably gay subject matter was typically limited, in part because of visibility — as in not willing to announce or flaunt one's sexuality — and in part because much of the iconography of mainstream tattooing, with all its myriad variations, often speaks to a larger consciousness common to all of us.

I happened to be in the right place at the right time. The 1970s through the 1990s was an intense period during which gay people across the country were becoming galvanized, rebelling against a deadly status quo, and starting to loudly demand equality and respect with an unprecedented and infectious spirit of defiance and pride. The AIDS epidemic hit the gay community like a hurricane. On the one hand, the advent of AIDS meant that gays were targeted even more viciously, especially by religious conservatives. On the other hand, AIDS strengthened the resolve of a minority not to be treated as second-class citizens, not to be viewed as Evil in Levi's, not to be denied the same human rights enjoyed by the rest of American society.

Tattooing is about people — and a story like this can only be forged by the people whose lives have intertwined with mine, people who have come and gone, each having brought a bit of a rainbow, like different-colored yarns in a fantastic tapestry.

While working on this memoir, digging through distant memories, I would find myself suddenly recalling some little thing out of the blue that I hadn't thought of in years — an inconsequential reflection of an old neon sign in the wet sidewalk, for instance, or that the Zuni Café on Market Street served a really pleasant grapefruit ice, or the smell of that old gym on Valencia Street.

Prologue: I Wake The Tattoo God

It was a nice day in Phoenix, Arizona, sometime in the fall or early winter, 1977, and my first lover and I had driven down to spend the day. As we were driving along, we spotted a nondescript little tattoo shop, and serendipitously decided right then to go in and get a tattoo.

When we got inside there was one person behind the counter, a youngish guy, and I noted with interest that he was reading a biography of Philip II of Spain. We perused the flash on the walls, selected a small design, and proceeded to get it tattooed on our ass cheeks.

When we got back in the car, I commented something like, "Why on earth would someone intelligent enough to be reading about Philip II of Spain be doing tattoos?"

Oh, man, I must have really stuck my foot in it. The Tattoo God tilted his head a bit, raised an eyebrow, and thought to himself, "OK, smart-ass, you're gonna find out."

I had no clue what was coming down the pike for me.

COMING OUT

By the time I was six years old both of my parents had died, and my half-sister and I had been adopted by my maternal grandparents. They were typical hard-working, blue-collar products of the Great Depression. Sometimes I wonder how difficult it must have been for them, or for anyone in their early 50s for that matter, to take on two youngsters to raise. They had valuable wisdom to share that the parents of my peers didn't have, but at the same time it was a little like living in a time warp. I didn't really have any friends my age that I would spend time with outside of school.

My grandfather wasn't a religious man. My grandmother, however, must have felt that we kids shouldn't miss out on God even though she didn't go to church, so every Sunday we were dropped off at the local Mormon ward and picked up after services.

Growing up Mormon in small-town Arizona — or anywhere else, actually — is hardly a path to healthy self-esteem if you're a gay kid. The standard recipe is to deny who and what you are and accept for a fact that God thinks you're unworthy of his love, or much of anything else, unless you change.

Even masturbation was a subject for serious heavenly concern, with strange and useless suggestions by church Elders for keeping oneself out of temptation's path; for instance, never being nude except to quickly bathe and change clothes, and avoiding unsavory types who might encourage such self-destructive behavior. In the 1970s, Mark E. Peterson, a member of the Council of the Twelve Apostles, even recommended a form of aversion therapy by suggesting that "if you are tempted to masturbate, think of having to bathe in a tub of worms, and eat several of them as you do the act."[1]

But attractions are what they are. I would start feeling all funny inside watching young actor James MacArthur in the Disney films *The Light In The Forest* and *Kidnapped*. There were a couple of boys at school who were achingly handsome. On television there was Guy Madison, star of *The Adventures of Wild Bill Hickok*. Richard Chamberlain as *Dr. Kildare* made me melt inside. Even the boys' underwear ads in the Sears catalog held my secret, prurient attention despite being obviously retouched so as not to show a bulge.

I didn't understand the why of these attractions, and I certainly didn't mention them to anyone. Schoolmates spoke derisively of "queers" and "fags." Same-sex attractions were anathema as far as the church was concerned. Furthermore, the only men I knew for sure were gay were old, sad, effeminate lechers that gave me the creeps. So, teen logic what it is, I brilliantly concluded that because I wasn't like them, then obviously I wasn't "that way."

Throughout my teens I explored art on my own, studying oil painting from Walter T. Foster "How-To" books. But my special joy was charcoal figure drawing. I had acquired a

---

[1]Mark E. Peterson, "Mormon Masturbation Prevention," Moonlight Mac, http://www.moonmac.com/Mormon_masturbation.html.

couple of paperback figure drawing instruction books by the renowned teacher George Bridgman, and I carefully worked through them. Admittedly, there was an erotic element to figure drawing, but I kept that to myself. I never had the nerve to ask anyone to pose for me. My larger artistic interest at the time was music, perhaps in part because I didn't know any working artists who might have been inspirational.

By my senior year of high school, I had begun seriously questioning my religion, and there were lots of things that simply didn't add up for me. By the time I started college, I had left the church behind. I was still convinced, though, that I wasn't "queer," and I got married in my junior year of college.

My first actual gay experiences happened after college graduation while I was in the Army, stationed in Germany. Decades before "Don't ask, don't tell" (DADT) became the official United States policy on gays serving in the military, it was already understood among queer service members as an unwritten rule. When I started graduate studies after my discharge, I continued furtive encounters on the down-low, having discovered the real purpose of "glory holes" in the university library men's room.

In 1975 and 1976, after earning a Master's degree, I attended the American Conservatory at Fontainebleau, France, about a half-hour train ride south of Paris, where I studied piano and composition with the legendary teacher Nadia Boulanger. My secretive sexual encounters continued there, too, often with young French military personnel who came from the next town over to cruise for tricks in the extensive palace gardens. Another place to meet anonymous sex partners was the street-accessible restroom built into the wall of the Catholic church adjacent to where the twice-weekly outdoor markets were held.

One day I went up to Paris to get away from the school and visit the Louvre. While sipping espresso at a sidewalk café, I spotted a young gay couple strolling along the river Seine holding hands. I recall feeling terribly envious of their apparent freedom as well as feeling a bit trapped in my current situation.

The trouble was I didn't feel good about my dishonesty, not only to my wife, but to myself. Lying to yourself and to everyone around you is like standing under the shower and convincing yourself you're not wet. Things were not getting any easier, either, because by the mid-1970s homosexuality was certainly in the news.

In December, 1973, spurred by studies by Evelyn Hooker, the American Psychiatric Association expunged homosexuality from its list of mental disorders.

The 1974 novel *Front Runner* by Patricia Nell Warren was a tear-jerker of a love story and was the first book of contemporary gay fiction to be on the *New York Times* Best Seller List.

In September, 1975, the cover of *Time* magazine featured Air Force sergeant Leonard Matlovich. He was the first American Armed Services member to publicly challenge the military's anti-gay policies.

In December of that same year, retired NFL player David Kopay became the first major athlete to come out as gay. Along with coauthor Perry Deane Young, Kopay published his 1977 biography, *The David Kopay Story*.

In 1977 John Rechy published *The Sexual Outlaw*, a non-fiction work detailing the devastating effects of homophobia, especially entrapment of homosexuals by law-enforcement agencies.

Across America, especially in small-town and rural areas, *The Advocate* was the primary vehicle for gay news, politics, opinion pieces, and arts and entertainment. First published in 1967, *The Advocate* arrived in a plain brown envelope, in a small newspaper format.

But none of these things galvanized national attention to gay issues in the way that singer, beauty pageant winner, and Florida Orange Juice spokesperson Anita Bryant brought about. In 1977 Dade County passed an ordinance prohibiting discrimination on the basis of sexual orientation. Bryant became the head of, and chief spokesperson for, a coalition named Save Our Children, stating, "I will lead such a crusade to stop it as this country has not seen before." Her efforts were successful, and the anti-discrimination ordinance was repealed by a wide margin.

What nobody expected, however, was the highly visible Florida Citrus boycott backlash from the gay community and a host of celebrities that included Barbra Streisand, Bette Midler, Carroll O'Connor, and Mary Tyler Moore. Gay bars across the country removed screwdrivers from their menus, replacing them with a cocktail made of vodka and apple juice named "the Anita Bryant." Pins, badges, and bumper stickers proclaimed the boycott, and I put one of the bumper stickers on my VW beetle.

The great irony is that Bryant's hatred and highly public vitriol brought gay issues to national prominence. In his now famous "Hope Speech," Harvey Milk pointed out that, "For the first time in the history of the world, everybody was talking about it, good or bad...more about the word homosexual and gay was written than probably in the history of mankind."[2]

In a strange kind of karmic justice, Bryant and her manager/husband Bob Greene divorced soon after. Bob Greene remained reclusive and bitter for the remainder of his life, hating and blaming gays for his failed marriage.[3]

At last I came to the wise and important conclusion that I wasn't the one with the problem. My growing openness, the boycott bumper sticker, plus the fact that I had gotten my left ear pierced were finally too much for my marriage. The resulting divorce was more or less amicable, and I was at last out of the closet — to my family, myself, and the world. I left everything behind except for my piano and some personal belongings, and moved in with my first lover.

During my graduate studies I had written a chamber concerto for harpsichord, and while studying in France I became increasingly interested in historic and contemporary

---

[2]Harvey Milk, "The Hope Speech," Danaroc.com, http://www.danaroc.com/guests_harveymilk_122208.html.

[3]Elinor J. Brecher and Steve Rothaus, "Bob Green, former DJ and ex-husband of Anita Bryant, dies at 80," *The Washington Post*, http://articles.washingtonpost.com/2012-02-23/national/35446061_1_gay-rights-ordinance-marriage-christian-love.

literature for harpsichord. Through a friend I learned of Margaret Fabrizio, who was teaching at Stanford University, so I sent her a copy of the chamber concerto. Her response was enthusiastic, and I decided that this was the musical direction for me. At the same time my new partner had accepted a business-consulting position in Palo Alto.

In the summer of 1978 we moved to California. I flew to San Jose, rented a car, and drove up to Palo Alto. I found an affordable, charming little house on Charleston Road that had a lovely back yard with a very large mission fig tree. After securing the lease and setting up bank accounts, I flew back to Arizona.

We loaded up a U-Haul truck, and I made the drive to Palo Alto while my partner finished up some business. This was a period of nationwide gasoline shortages, driven by political uncertainty and wavering oil production in Iran. There were long lines at filling stations, and some areas of the country imposed an odd/even plan on gasoline purchases, based on the last digit of the auto license plate. Maximum speed on the freeways was reduced to 55 mph. The moving truck we rented had a regulator on it that prohibited speeds in excess of 55 mph, so it took almost a day longer to arrive in Palo Alto than it would otherwise have taken. But we eventually got settled in, and I commenced my studies.

As a gift, my lover bought me a handsome harpsichord built by Jerry Prager in Los Angeles. It was a "French Double" — two keyboards and three ranks of strings, including an additional set of *peau de boeuf* jacks — leather quills made from cow hide.

I soon discovered that music for harpsichord, contemporary or historic, simply wasn't high on the list when it came to pursuing a doctoral degree at Stanford, unless it was in performance. In fact, the man who would have been my doctoral advisor stated flat out that the music department was far more interested in electronic computer-based music, pointing out that the famous Artificial Intelligence Lab was an unparalleled resource for composers. I began to realize that academia and I weren't really going to be a match made in heaven. However, I continued my coaching privately, believing that sooner or later the right combination of things would come along.

That September, on the last Sunday of the month, we drove up to visit a friend who suggested we take in the Castro Street Fair, which just happened to be taking place on that very day. We parked a couple of blocks away and walked to the Castro. Never had I seen so many gay men jammed together. There were thousands! Never had I experienced so many people so joyous, so determined to express themselves to the world. The feeling of pride was infectious — no shame, no guilt, no going back.

My interest in drawing and art hadn't really waned, and I had continued to dabble in one medium or another. Making art, though, was still a private pleasure. Significantly at this time, I was spending spare moments pursuing calligraphy, impressed by so many breathtaking examples I had seen in museums in Germany, France, and England. In retrospect, I sometimes wonder if the Tattoo God wasn't already plotting my comeuppance.

In November, 1978, gays throughout California celebrated the voter defeat of California Proposition 6, sponsored by John Briggs, who referred to San Francisco as the country's "moral garbage dump of homosexuality."[4] If it had been successful, the Briggs Initiative would have banned gays and lesbians from working in California's public schools, or as any public school employee who supported gay rights. Peculiarly, considering his later colossal lack of responsiveness to the AIDS crisis, former governor Ronald Reagan was among the politicians and celebrities, including then-governor Jerry Brown, who opposed the measure.

That happy glow didn't last very long. On November 27, 1978, news broke that San Francisco Mayor George Moscone and Supervisor Harvey Milk had been assassinated. News of the assassination flooded national TV stations, and that evening we watched moving footage of the enormous candle-light march in San Francisco.

My relationship with my first partner didn't last but a short while longer. He moved back to Arizona, and I sold my piano, packed up my harpsichord and meager belongings, and moved from Palo Alto to San Francisco in April, 1979, the month of my 32nd birthday.

---

[4]John Gallagher and Chris Bull, "Perfect Enemies: The Religious Right, the Gay Movement, and the Politics of the 1990s, Chapter 1: The Battle Lines Are Drawn," *The Washington Post*, http://www. washingtonpost.com/wp-srv/style/longterm/books/chap1/ perfectenemies.htm.

FRISCO

I had grown to love "the City." At last I felt that here was a place I could call home, a place where I could be my own man, where I could accomplish whatever was in me to accomplish. I loved the cityscapes, the panoramas, the fog, the exciting eclectic hubbub. I had found a roommate situation with a couple living on Walter Street, barely a half block from Duboce Park. It was only a short walk from the flat to Church Street Station, a popular coffee shop and bar at the corner of Church and Market, or to the Balcony bar, a few doors up from Church Street Station going toward Castro Street barely three blocks away.

My roommates introduced me to the *San Francisco Chronicle* and the daily columns of Herb Caen, whom everybody followed avidly for his witty stories, quips, and insights into the popular culture of his beloved "Baghdad by the Bay." The other must-read was Armistead Maupin's *Tales of the City* in its serialized form. They also introduced me to the *Bay Area Reporter (B.A.R.)*, a free weekly newspaper serving the LGBT communities in the Bay Area.

Thanks in part to Herb Caen, I also learned about what I can only call the "please don't call it Frisco" syndrome. There are actually people who become offended and who act as though they'll be scarred for life if you refer to San Francisco by any other name. Never mind that the nickname "Frisco" harks clear back to the Gold Rush and the Barbary Coast Era and for me, at least, conjures up visions of a wild town where all manner of things took place — from tent cities during the Gold Rush, to being shanghaied, to dangerous waterfront bars, to busy brick brothels, to wandering in dark foggy alleys just like Bogey in *The Maltese Falcon*. **That** was Frisco.

I loved the City's quirkiness, with all its odd characters one encountered daily. Here was a city that not only tolerated its eccentric citizens but tended to treasure them — everything from the evangelist at Market and Powell who dragged around a big wooden cross with a wheel on the end, to the narcissistic photographer, model, and artist Armin Hagen Freiherr von Hoyningen-Huene, better known as Peter Berlin. Now and then on our way to and from work or heading to the Castro, we would observe an elderly lady walking along Market Street who stopped at every phone booth along the way to check the coin box for change. I named her "Penny Annie."

Living so close to the Castro, I would head that way to do my simple shopping and, of course, cruise the bars. A bottle of Budweiser was 75 cents. That may seem paltry now, but the minimum hourly wage in California in 1979 was $2.90.[5]

Almost no gay bar served Coors because of a boycott stemming from accusations that Coors had fired gay and lesbian employees. The boycott went on for some time. To its credit, in May 1995 Coors became the 21st publicly-traded U.S. corporation to extend employee benefits to same-sex partners.

The new gay sensibility had almost universally adopted

---

[5]Author unknown, "History of California Minimum Wage," California Department of Industrial Relations, http://www.dir. ca.gov/iwc/minimumwagehistory.htm.

an idealized blue-collar working-man look consisting of shrink-to-fit Levi 501's with the famous button fly, plaid shirts, and engineer or western boots, along with a short hair style, mustache, and sideburns. It wasn't uncommon for guys to use sandpaper on their Levi's to highlight strategic spots. What came to be called the "Castro Clone" look became ubiquitous, spreading from San Francisco to New York, Berlin, Amsterdam, and other major cities with large gay populations.

This was also the height of the disco era, and San Francisco was a major force in shaping the disco dance craze worldwide. Gay boys flocked to venues like the Trocadero Transfer, and vocal artists Sylvester (James) and "Two Tons O' Fun" Izora Rhodes were local disco icons. The disco group Village People captured the essence of the hyper-masculine with hits like "Macho Man," "Y.M.C.A," "In The Navy," and "Go West." The campy classic "It's Raining Men" by The Weather Girls regularly blared out over the crowd.

In "Gay Mecca," however, the threat of gay bashing and even death were a very real hazard we all lived with, spurred in part by the vitriol spewing from anti-gay crusaders like Anita Bryant and John Briggs. Just two years previously, on June 21, 1977, a gardener named Robert Hillsborough died from 15 stab wounds while his attacker yelled "Faggot!"[6]

Because of the violence directed toward gays I learned

---

[6]Author unknown, "Robert Hillsborough," Gay History Wiki: A History Discovered, http://gayhistory.wikidot.com/robert-hillsborough.

about the Butterfly Brigade (Castro Street Safety Patrol) and the Carry A Whistle Defense Campaign, founded in 1976 by gay activist Henry "Hank" Wilson. We were all urged to carry whistles that we could use in the event of being attacked. On weekends, during critical hours, Butterfly Brigade volunteers armed with portable walkie-talkies manned street corners in the Castro and along Market Street, ready to respond if someone should start blowing his whistle. It was actually fairly effective because everyone within earshot would respond by blowing his whistle and hurrying to the place where trouble was happening. Gay-owned and gay-friendly shops throughout the City carried whistles made of metal or brightly-colored plastic, and virtually every gay man had a whistle on his keychain. I carried my whistle for years until my keychain finally wore through the metal loop on the whistle. I still have that whistle.

I had been in the City scarcely over a month when, on May 21, ex-cop, ex-fireman, and ex-supervisor Dan White was convicted of voluntary manslaughter for the shooting murders of San Francisco Mayor George Moscone and gay Supervisor Harvey Milk. The City was stunned that, based on what came to be called the "Twinkie Defense," a sentence of only 7 years, 8 months was handed down for the blatant murders of two people. By early that evening a crowd had gathered at Castro and Market, and as the crowd grew, traffic came to a standstill and TV news trucks arrived, along with the police. News traveled fast, and my roommates and I received several telephone calls telling us what was going on.

The crowd began moving down Market Street toward City Hall, becoming larger, louder, and angrier. My roommates and I joined up with it at Church Street. By the time the crowd reached the Civic Center it had become huge. Some people near the entrance to City Hall yanked wrought iron grillwork off the doors and used it to smash glass and windows. Someone managed to start a fire inside. Even though police stood by in riot gear, they weren't allowed to respond. Numerous police cars were torched, and stores along Market Street were being vandalized.

Easily claustrophobic in crowds, I elected to stay along the edges. I didn't like the ugly temperament I saw taking place, so I left the crowd and began walking back, as had others. What we didn't see was that the police were finally given permission to respond, and battles between police and protesters erupted everywhere. Police retaliation was vicious. After regrouping at 18th and Castro, almost three miles from Civic Center, they completely trashed the Elephant Walk bar and savagely beat anyone they could grab.

The very next day after the riot was Harvey Milk's birthday, and the planned celebration on Castro took place even though heavily surveilled by police. Dan White served only 5 years of his term. Two years after his release, unable to start over and forced to hide, he committed suicide in his garage by carbon monoxide poisoning.

Along with the turmoil that engulfed the gay community, my financial situation was equally troubling, and I knew I would have to find a job. Of all things, I got hired at a vasectomy clinic on Sutter Street, where a retired doctor came in three days a week for the procedures. The clientele were largely blue-collar and lower-income guys who either already had enough children or were simply concerned about never being a parent. Their initial knowledge of the procedure was scant at best, and some even feared that getting a vasectomy might make them gay. I didn't assist with the actual surgeries. Instead, I booked appointments, sterilized instrument packs, maintained consent forms, answered questions, and did the live-sperm exams.

Following a vasectomy it takes about 10-12 days for a man's tubes to be clear of "swimmers." The patient must bring in a sample ejaculate for examination under a microscope. If there are still any little wiggly guys, the patient must avoid unprotected sex until there are none visible. Although we provided a small plastic portion cup for them to bring in their ideally fresh sample, we also had a small private room with stimulating reading material for commuters and the like who couldn't conveniently carry the portion cup.

The clinic had a unique T-shirt. The image on the front featured a large pair of oranges labeled "Funkist." Below the oranges was the phrase "All of the Juice, None of the Seed." It was so tacky! I wish now that I had had the presence of mind to keep at least one.

Business at the vasectomy clinic had been in decline even before I started working there. I kept telling the doctor and clinic manager that they should move their business across the Bay because, clearly, there simply wasn't a sufficient population base interested in vasectomies at their current location. About four months after I started working there, the business closed and I needed to find another job.

The Castro district, while the center of local gay politics, epitomized a middle-class mindset despite the outwardly hyper-masculine overtones. There was another district, however, that my roommates and acquaintances talked about, mostly in terms of a place to be avoided because it was for "serious" leathermen and bikers and other tough types (Oh, My!). Folsom Street! South of Market! To go there was to really take a walk on the wild side. So of course, like Alice, I became curioser and curioser.

There was naturally some overlap. The Castro did have one small leather shop, and that was my initial introduction to a world I had only heard or read about. I bought a modest leather vest. I remember feeling somewhat intimidated when I saw guys that were obviously more hard-core, but at the same time I couldn't help feeling intrigued.

A stretch of Folsom Street, from 12th Street to 3rd Street, was known as the Miracle Mile, and here was the real sub-cultural sexual center of the City. By day, the South of Market (SOMA) was mostly small business and manufacturing — metal plating, plastics, electrical repair shops, small automotive repair shops, a cardboard barrel and burlap bag distributor, even a casket builder. There was an assortment of empty factories, including the remains of a Falstaff beer brewery at 10th and Harrison. Scattered among the businesses were modest Victorian-style homes converted to flats that attracted artists because rents were not only cheaper, but the City had zoned the area for artist live-work spaces.

By evening, however, the atmosphere changed, and hundreds of men poured into the area. From Hamburger Mary's and The Eagle bar on 12th Street all the way to the Ritch Street Baths on 3rd Street, there were bars and sex clubs such as The Bolt, The Stud, Fe-Be's, The Ramrod, The Watering Hole, the Arena, the Ambush, The Slot, the Handball Express, and the 8th Street Baths — all within a short walk from one to the other. Random anonymous sex was easily available and frequent. Not only did many of the bars have active back rooms, but the dark secluded alleys were ready-made for furtive encounters. The average age range was wider here, too. Men over 40 were hardly considered over the hill in this world.

I applied for a minimum-wage sales job at A Taste Of Leather on Folsom Street. Located between 5th and 6th Streets at the time, it was advertised as the largest gay leather store in the country, occupying a warehouse-sized space. It was solely owned and operated by a horrible old man who called himself Nick O'Demus. Like a character from a lost Charles Dickens novel, he rarely bathed, sported a scraggly beard, kept his hair in a greasy pony tail, and always wore the same smelly Army Surplus fatigues. He had a taste for young hustlers whom he would pick up along a section of Polk Street referred to as "Polk Gulch." As an employer he was demanding and paranoid, certain that everybody was intent on stealing him blind.

Nick occupied the second floor of the business, where he slept in a dirty old bed amid piles of papers, stained jock straps, assorted unwashed socks, and fast-food containers. On the same upper floor is where employees clocked in for work beside a small table with a wretched little coffee maker. The only toilet was downstairs, so rather than trek downstairs at night, Nick would pee in a round apple juice bottle and add it to dozens of others on a narrow shelf that ran along the walls. Despite his quirks, Nick was a rather shrewd business man, and I learned some things about retail marketing that would benefit me later on.

For a guy who had grown up in small-town Arizona, A Taste Of Leather was a wonderland. I discovered magazines like *Drummer* (1975-1999), devoted to gay leather lifestyle stories, photos, and personal ads. *Straight To Hell*, also known as *The Manhattan Review Of Unnatural Acts*, was a cheaply-printed hip-pocket periodical featuring real reader-submitted sex histories and raunchy photos, edited by cult New York writer Boyd McDonald. There was a product for almost any fetish, including the Accu-Jac, a mechanical blowjob machine that looked more like some ghastly equipment you might expect to find in a horror-movie ambulance. There was leather clothing, bondage gear, sex toys, greeting cards, and a complete selection of bandanas in a wide variety of colors. The color of the bandana, carried in the right or left hip pocket, indicated to others what variety of sexual activity someone was into, and whether or not he was "bottom" or "top."

I was able to get a genuine California Highway Patrol (CHP) motorcycle jacket for less than half price because there was a rip in the lining, and Nick complained that he couldn't sell it for full price.

Nick's personality quirks, however weird, weren't sufficient to overshadow larger gay concerns. The first

National March on Washington for Lesbian and Gay Rights took place that October, drawing between 75,000 and 125,000 people demanding equal civil rights. The march served to nationalize issues of gay equality including sexual orientation discrimination by the Federal Government.[7]

That same October I went to the Halloween celebration in the Castro. Sometimes called "gay Mardi Gras," it was among the leading Halloween celebrations in the country, drawing massive crowds and featuring outrageous costumes and entertainment. During the entire month of October my roommates had worked on their outfits. I'm not a particularly costume-type of person but decided to take in some of the festivities anyway. In the early evening I walked to Church Street Station to have a meal before heading up that way.

While I was dining an acquaintance came up to my table and joined me. He was in drag, wearing a black cocktail dress and high heels. He asked me if I would accompany him up to Castro Street because he was feeling rather vulnerable, so I agreed. He had no jacket in spite of the cool evening air, so I let him wear my newly-acquired leather motorcycle jacket over his shoulders.

That 3-block walk was a startling revelation in just how hateful people can be. As we left Church Street Station, Market Street was busy with traffic — mostly taxis and gawkers. Many of the cars, usually carrying 3 or more

---

[7]Rick Landman, "First March on Washington for Lesbian and Gay Rights was held on October 14, 1979," Infotrue Educational Experiences, http://www.infotrue.com/wash.html.

persons, drove along slowly, while the people inside stared and pointed and yelled epithets. Some threw bottles, rocks, or green apples at obviously gay pedestrians. By the time we reached Noe Street I decided we should get off of Market, so we went down Noe Street to 17th Street and from there proceeded to Castro. Not liking close crowds I was uncomfortable, so after an hour or so I gave my friend cab fare to get home safely and made my way back to Walter Street. I never again went to another Castro Street Halloween.

I worked at A Taste of Leather for only three months. During my timed 45-minute lunch breaks I would go to The Watering Hole bar just up the street where I could get a hot dog and a beer because I couldn't afford much more. When I would return to work Nick groused that I drank my lunch. I should have! One morning when I got to work, Nick ordered me to wash up a sink-full of filthy dildos he had used the night before. I refused, and that was that. The Tattoo God smiled to himself, though, because now he almost had me where he wanted me. I didn't see anything great about it though, because Christmas was approaching and I was out of a job.

Around mid-day on Christmas Eve, I talked my roommates into a plot. We headed down Market Street to about Dolores Street, where we spotted Penny Annie on her daily sojourn. Staying about a half-block ahead of her all the way to Castro, we put dimes or quarters in the phone booth change boxes for her to find.

My next two jobs were unremarkable. One was at a sandwich shop where I was paid under the table, followed by a swing-shift gig working for the San Francisco Municipal Railway (MUNI). I had moved to a 3-story apartment complex on Grove Street, between Divisadero and Scott Streets, adjacent to Alamo Square, where I enjoyed a reduced rent in exchange for light building maintenance. That wasn't too bad, and I didn't have to collect rent. I kept the hallways vacuumed and the windows washed. What I hated, though, was cleaning up the trash area, because the 3-story high garbage chute was always jammed with smelly paper bags, cardboard, loose garbage, and dirty diapers. Ugh!

I continued to study and practice the harpsichord, giving a couple of small recitals. I had become quite fond of harpsichord literature of the French Baroque, with a focus on the works of Jean-Philippe Rameau and François Couperin. In a seemingly strange juxtaposition I was also avidly devouring the writings of French author Jean Genet, particularly *The Miracle of the Rose*, *The Thief's Journal*, *Our Lady of the Flowers*, and *Querelle de Brest*.

At the August, 1980 National Convention, The Democratic Party became the first political party to endorse a homosexual rights platform.[8] In November Ronald Reagan was elected as the 40th President of the United States. Even before Reagan was elected, *The Advocate* was warning readers about the former California governor, who had referred to gay people as "sick unfortunates" and who,

---

[8]Author unknown, "WGBH American Experience, Stonewall Uprising," American Experience: 25 Years, http://www.pbs.org/wgbh/americanexperience/features/timeline/stonewall.

in the 1970s, had stalled repeal of California's anti-sodomy laws.[9]

---

[9]A Gentleman, "Hate Lives Here," A Gentleman's View, http://agentlemansview.com/hate-lives-here.

THE AMBUSH

Sometimes there's a wrinkle in life's fabric, as though time is suspended somehow and a magical element pervades everything. Sometimes it's only for a very little while, sometimes longer, but the effect is that of being granted a special and privileged glimpse into another reality, like one of those parallel universes postulated in string theory.

In 1981, through a friend, I grabbed at the opportunity to work at the Ambush bar. Now the Tattoo God was really pleased with himself. He smiled his enigmatic smile, and his eyes twinkled.

The Ambush, between 9th and 10th streets on Harrison and about a half block from an abandoned Falstaff beer brewery, was different from any of the other South of Market bars. Referred to by regulars simply as "The 'Bush," the difference was palpable from the moment you pushed aside the black leather curtain covering the entrance and stepped inside. The eclectic music was subdued compared to other bars. The walls were a deep, rich, cool gray instead of the typical dull matte black. There was genuine art on the walls, and centered behind the bar there was always a huge floral arrangement in front of a gigantic mirror. At the far end by the back exit was a free-standing, cast-iron gas stove/fireplace — a comfort on cold rainy nights.

At the street end, high up the wall, was a window space with a large exhaust fan which allowed harsh sunlight to pour into the bar in the afternoons. To solve that problem, someone had constructed a metal frame in which were suspended dozens of old chandelier crystals, and so every afternoon the entire bar would be filled with rainbows. The bar lighting had been cleverly designed to maintain that rainbow effect.

To get a sense of the effect, think of the Toulouse-Lautrec painting *Au Moulin Rouge*. You could grab a handful of peanuts from the big wooden barrel next to the cast-iron stove, park your butt on one of the "meat racks" (benches built with storage for beer cases underneath), fire up a joint, sip on a beer, and chat with friends or cruise the hot guys, or both. By closing time the floor was littered at least an inch deep with joint "roaches," cigarette butts, and peanut shells. The last-call music tape was always the same, starting with "Why Don't We Get Drunk And Screw" (Jimmy Buffet), followed by "The Y'all Come Back Saloon" (Oak Ridge Boys).

Compared to the other South of Market bars, the Ambush attracted a more relaxed and laid back assortment of hippie bikers, leather/Levi types, guys in business suits just getting off work, intellectuals, and just plain ordinary guys in jeans and t-shirts. In short it was a stoner bar, serving only beer and wine — no hard liquor. There were three owners: Kerry Bowman, David Delay, and Kenny Ferguson. Kerry was the principal manager, whom everyone affectionately called Miss Kitty — a reference to actress Amanda Blake's character of the same name who ran Dodge City's Long Branch Saloon in the TV series "Gunsmoke." Kerry promoted a vision of the bar as theater, and always referred to the patrons as "guests." And it worked. On weekends the line of motorcycles parked out front extended more than half a block.

The building, located at the corner of Harrison Street and Dore Alley, was a typical San Francisco Victorian-style with three floors. The building owner was a kindly old guy who didn't seem to mind that the business took over all three floors and kept remodeling. While the main bar was on the first floor, there was a small "deli" on the second floor where you could get a quite decent meal. Adjacent to the deli was a small leather shop that also sold Ambush Poppers, real amyl nitrate made for the Ambush by a local chemist in his basement. Besides storage the third floor had a staff lounge, a small kitchen, and a leather production area with three industrial sewing machines, a huge work table, and other equipment.

The Toulouse-Lautrec comparison didn't end with the bar's visual atmosphere. In many ways the Ambush echoed the free-wheeling bohemian lifestyle of Paris' Montmartre district of the 1880s-1890s, which not only provided entertainment, but was also the haunt of intellectuals, artists, writers, philosophers, and musicians.

The list of people who came into the 'Bush was a small who's-who of the San Francisco gay community:

- prize-winning poet and Guggenheim fellow Thom Gunn;

- biochemist Geoff Mains, author of the groundbreaking book *Urban Aboriginals: A Celebration of Leather Sexuality* (1984);

- gay radical sex photographer Mark I. Chester;

- photographers Robert Pruzan and Jim Wigler;

- playwright Robert Chesley;

- *Drummer* editor Jack Fritscher, PhD, who, along with his lover Robert Mapplethorpe, shot art videos of two Ambush owners, David Delay and Kerry Bowman; in 1984 the Ambush hosted the launch of two leather books by Fritscher;

- author Race Bannon, widely acknowledged and award-winning expert on alternative sexuality;

- Dr. Gayle Rubin, author of *Thinking Sex: Notes for a Radical Theory of the Politics of Sexuality*, considered to be one of the major works of pro-sex feminism;

- Pat (now Patrick) Califia, who, along with Gayle Rubin, was one of the founders of Samois, the first lesbian sadomasochism group;

- musician and composer Peter Hartman;

- Los Angeles-based psychotherapist, author, activist, and educator Guy Baldwin;

- famed South of Market artist/muralist Chuck Arnett, who had designed the Ambush logo and flag;

- bartender/artist Bill Tellman, Chuck Arnett's lover, whose art appeared on many event posters and who designed the intricate lettering for the Ambush logo.

Among the bar regulars were members of the Rainbow Motorcycle Club, a gay men's motorcycle club originally founded in 1971. The RMC was a radical departure from other motorcycle clubs in that there was no charter, no constitution, no officers, and no membership dues. Instead it was an informal group of gay men with an extraordinarily talented membership equally at home discussing one-act plays of Samuel Beckett, the minuscule works of Austrian composer Anton Webern, or favorite raunchy sex practices.

Other bars held events like Sunday beer busts, bare chest contests, or slave auctions for charities. But not the Ambush. By contrast, there was a new art show every month featuring work by outstanding gay artists from around California and beyond. Usually the shows featured the work of a single individual, and the openings were well-attended, gala affairs, complete with special music chosen to complement the art works, and gourmet hors d'oeuvres prepared in the 3rd-floor kitchen.

Our artist-in-residence was Glenn Alan Zehrbaugh, a long-haired, bearded hippie in his 50s who went by the name Snowflake. His paintings and drawings chronicled the South of Market area of the 70s and 80s, from street scenes to portraits to interior scenes of the Ambush, and his art shows regularly sold out, often before they were mounted. He was a bit of a curmudgeon, but Snowflake and I came to be fast friends. We frequently talked about art and art history. We also had fun making up names for colors, mocking the color names of major paint companies: "Fruit Compote," "Drag Queen Pink," "Ham," "Jock Strap," "Baby's First Summer," etc. Snowflake methodically took photos of his paintings on the roof of his apartment building. Those photos are now in the collection of the ONE Archive in Los Angeles.

Thanksgiving was particularly festive at the 'Bush because it marked the anniversary of its opening in 1974. Everyone was invited, including many of the area's homeless residents; and the layout was lavish. The pool table groaned under the weight of food lighted by enormous silver candelabras. And nobody passed up the acid punch (LSD) that practically glowed in a huge crystal punchbowl near the far end of the bar.

The Ambush was a special little niche of the South of Market Sexual Outlaw subculture. The regulars seldom went to any of the other bars. There was simply no need to go anywhere else. If you were lucky enough to work there, were creative, and had the balls to go for it, you could be assured of encouragement and support from the owners, the staff, and the regulars. I started in the deli, serving up sandwiches, soups, and salads, as well as hors d'oeuvres for the art shows.

Several of the Ambush crew, like many seasoned South of Market regulars, tended to look down on perceived newbies and the inexperienced. One of these was Norman, who tended the front bar most evenings. Norman had lost most of the toes on his right foot, which made him popular with certain sex fetishists. I had only been working there a couple of days or so when, at the end of a deli shift, I went downstairs to the bar to have a beer. Norman looked down his nose at me, curled up his lip, and spat at me. That pissed me off, so I spat back at him and demanded, "Give me a beer." In Norman's mind I was now OK, not only because I didn't back down, but because I asked for Ranier ale which, unbeknownst to me, was his personal favorite, and which the staff had dubbed "Green Death" because of the color of the bottle.

Because I could draw and had continued practicing calligraphy in my spare time, I began making the signs for deli menus and specials. Before long I was also making signs and labels for the leather shop and art shows.

For a break I would sometimes head directly across the street to Juanita's, a Mexican cantina operated by a woman named Dolores. She was a delightful, chubby soul who in her younger days had been a quite stunning flamenco dancer. Now and then she would come across the street to get change. The interior of Juanita's was plain, with some old posters and music emanating from a crackling radio. Dolores would serve up her special mescal from a private source in Mexico. We always suspected Dolores had a couple of girls who took care of certain customers upstairs, because from the third floor of the Ambush we could look across the street into an upstairs room, where the action was accompanied by a grainy old black-and-white porn video that never changed. Later on, following the 1989 Loma Prieta earthquake, Juanita's became the Lone Star Saloon.

There were certainly a lot of handsome guys at the bar, but the Ambush also seemed to have more than its fair share of odd characters. There was "Piglet," a skinny guy who wrote political stuff on his perpetually less-than-clean tank tops; the guy whom nobody liked because he was always asking if you wanted to smell his finger; a somewhat surly red-headed giant who always wore green corduroy coveralls and looked for all the world like a garden-gnome-gone-bad fresh out of prison; cross-eyed Patrick, who did morning cleanup and worked as a bar back and who was always in some kind of trouble but the owners didn't have the heart to fire him.

Almost every day that it wasn't raining there was a homeless person who hung out along our block of Harrison Street. To describe him as disheveled would be kind. He was nick-named "Animal" because of his wild appearance and crazy behavior. In the mornings he would rummage through our dumpsters in Dore Alley, looking for food thrown out from the deli, even eating raw bacon. He would sit on the sidewalk in front of Juanita's and periodically beat the sidewalk with a plastic soft drink bottle, talking to himself and yelling at no one in particular. When he tired of that he would go into the phone booth at the corner of 10th and Harrison and alternately yell into the phone or bang the handset relentlessly against the phone box.

Despite his crazy carryings-on he was actually totally harmless. I felt sorry for Animal, so when I would look out the deli window and see him at the dumpster, I would often drop him a fresh sandwich and occasionally a pack of cigarettes. We believed he had a father somewhere who would periodically have Animal picked up and cleaned up, because he would reappear in a few days sporting a haircut, beard trim, and fresh clothes. Not that that did any good, really, but it was apparent that underneath all the grime was actually quite a good-looking man.

And then there was "Molly," a cab driver who made it a point to swing by the 'Bush several times a night. In her cab there was always a red leather rose on the dashboard. Flat-chested and plain, reminding one of Popeye's girlfriend Olive Oyl but with big glasses and bad teeth, Molly wished more than anything that she had been born a gay guy. She even wore a leather vest and a jock strap. But on her income she could never have afforded gender reassignment surgery. She was a staff favorite, and I have always wondered what became of her.

Working at the 'Bush made it possible for me to stay involved with my music. I became the harpsichordist with Lambda Pro Musica, a gay chamber orchestra founded by Jon Sims, who was also the founder of the San Francisco Gay Freedom Day Marching Band and Twirling Corps (now the San Francisco Lesbian/Gay Freedom Band) as well as the founder of the San Francisco Gay Men's Chorus. Lambda Pro Musica was an ambitious group, and we rehearsed frequently. I participated in the Baroque repertoire, performing such ambitious works as J. S. Bach's Fourth *Brandenburg* Concerto. I always performed wearing full leather with a red rose in the lapel of my motorcycle jacket.

I was honored to be a guest performer as part of the Gay Freedom Day Marching Band Christmas Concert at the Castro Theater, playing the celeste part for Tschaikovsky's "Dance of the Sugar Plum Fairy."

The great German director Rainer Fassbinder died a few months before the 1982 premiere of his last film, *Querelle*, based on Jean Genet's novel *Querelle de Brest*. What makes the film noteworthy here is that it was quite successful in spite of its strong homosexual thematic elements. The film was also a topic of discussion among some of the Ambush guests and myself.[10]

---

[10]Graham Russell, "Bitterness Personified: Reflections on Querelle (1982)," Bitterness Personified: Confessions of a Greaser Punk, http://graham-russell.blogspot.com/2011/07/reflections-on-querelle-1982.html.

THE DELUGE BEGINS

But in this halcyon bubble there was a creeping terror. In July, 1981, The *New York Times* printed the first story of a rare pneumonia and skin cancer found in 41 gay men in New York and California, and the news was echoed in the *Bay Area Reporter (B.A.R.)*. Whatever this was, it was causing people to waste away and die in what seemed like a matter of mere weeks. Some of these people were also getting purplish blotches on their skin, the telltale marks of Kaposi's Sarcoma.

Furthermore, it appeared to be happening only to gay people, and in fact the term "Gay Cancer" was the first description of it. A more official acronym was GRID — "Gay Related Immune Deficiency." AIDS (Acquired Immune Deficiency Syndrome) was first properly defined by the CDC in September, 1982. President Ronald Reagan said nothing publicly, even though it was clear that a major health crisis was developing.

But for most of us in the gay community, that news was like a ripple on the pond. What we didn't realize was that it was actually the fin of the shark that was to come.

I had a strict policy of never dating co-workers, but in one of the dumbest decisions of my life I ignored my own advice to date "Jim." In fact I moved in with Jim, and at his urging, we decided to leave San Francisco. We quit our jobs, loaded up his pickup truck, and headed off for Taos, New Mexico, where I became a chef in a vegetarian restaurant. How many ways can you spell "disaster?"

About three months after the move to Taos I returned to San Francisco. With my tail tucked between my legs I went to the 'Bush hoping against hope that I could get my job back.

One of the hazards of a somewhat pantheistic world view is that it's not always clear which god, or how many gods, should receive blame or praise for things. That's just as well, I suppose, because most gods are only interested in the praise part anyway, with the more demanding ones insisting on things like expensive virgin sacrifices. Suffice it to say I lucked out, didn't have to sacrifice any virgins or small animals, and was put to work sewing leather for the leather shop.

I took a studio apartment on Isis Street, at the corner of 12th Street between the Eagle bar and Hamburger Mary's, a short walk from the Ambush. The previous tenant was an Ambush regular we knew as "Crazy Richard." When I moved in the apartment walls had dozens of nail holes along with baseball-sized marks and depressions in the wallboard because Richard would have episodes of yelling and banging his head on the walls. One night, when police arrived in response to calls from neighbors, Richard explained to them that he was upset about his electricity bill. During the entire time I lived there, the landlord never did repair the walls.

Over at the Ambush, I worked with one other person, Rich Plum, and we enjoyed our own little world on the top floor. On the radio we listened to classical music until mid-afternoon, then switched to a country station. Besides the usual items, we made leather bow ties for the opening of the

Opera season, and used scrap leather to make beautifully-quilted sofa pillows in time for the holidays. Rich was an artist in his own right and played bassoon with the Gay Freedom Day Marching Band. He had created a line of leather backpacks for the shop that were quite popular, and it was Rich, along with Snowflake, who began encouraging me to pay more attention to my drawing skills.

Every gay leather business offered biker-style chaps, but the Ambush chaps were unique in several respects. The belt, instead of going all the way around the chaps, consisted of two pieces riveted at the hips. All seams were French seams, a much stronger construction. The legs featured welted edges and large zippers. We branded the belt with the Ambush logo. I made my own chaps and matching vest using a very dark chocolate-brown "Rolls Royce" leather, with black leather piping and black U.S. Cavalry-style leather bands going down the outside of the legs.

The Tattoo God was continuing to work in mysterious ways. Practically around the corner, on 9th street, the famed tattooer Cliff Raven had opened a San Francisco branch of Tattoo Works. He had become friends with porn-noir artist REX, and REX drew an advertising flyer for him.

I met Cliff when he came to the leather shop to have an armband crafted. He was an engaging, pleasant fellow, and we talked for some time. In 1960s Chicago, Cliff had been taught tattooing by iconic gay author Sam Steward aka "Phil Sparrow" who suggested Cliff bill himself as "Cliff Raven." I began to think I wanted another tattoo.

Now Cliff wasn't always at the shop. So on the day I

went in to see him, I was greeted instead by a guy named Phil Payton. A New Hampshire native with a typically wry New England sense of humor, his hodgepodge of tattoos included hinges on his finger joints, and there was a dotted line around his neck with the phrase "Cut Here."

For the first time I had an opportunity to actually watch the process. The placement I had chosen was on my left deltoid, and I recall precisely how Phil gripped my arm from the underside in order to stretch the skin. Even as a kid, I was never squeamish about needles or blood, so I watched with interest as he first outlined the piece, then methodically filled in the colors, frequently wiping away what seemed like copious amounts of excess ink mixed with a little blood.

Phil finished my tattoo, bandaged me up, and I went back to work. The Tattoo God was quite satisfied with himself — smug even — the seed had been planted. A short time later I got another tattoo which I had asked my friend, porn-noir artist REX, to design. It was two hearts connected by a lock, with flowers and the phrase "True Love." I loved the romantic sentiment of that tattoo.

One could also get body piercings at Cliff's shop, done by a handsome, tattooed guy named Peter Morrison. Peter was associated with the Gauntlet, the Los Angeles piercing establishment operated by Jim Ward. Not only did I get tattooed at the shop, Peter also installed my nipple rings.

I still didn't give any serious thought to tattooing or art. In my mind I was a musician who had to work to make ends meet. That same year (1982) I gave a harpsichord recital at the performance space 544 Natoma, brainchild of musician/composer Peter Hartman, with whom I had become good friends. It was to be my last public musical performance.

The fall of 1983, however, brought some major changes to my life. Being a romantic kind of guy, I wasn't nearly as promiscuous as most gay men in the City. There had been a series of boyfriends, but none had developed into a quality relationship. That is, until I met Tim, who would become my partner for the next 24 years. We met one evening at the 'Bush and, not long after, he moved into the little studio apartment with me, and we became a couple. Up until this time I had avoided getting a telephone, but now we had one.

We could not, however, register as domestic partners — a concept barely over a year old at the time. A 1982 version had been adopted and passed by the San Francisco Board of Supervisors, but it was vetoed by Mayor Dianne Feinstein. Many in the local gay community, feeling betrayed and outraged, joined with a group of White Panthers, who had mounted a recall election over her attempts to establish handgun controls. She handily beat the recall.[11]

In what was actually a wise business move, the owners of the 'Bush decided to end on-site production for the leather shop and move the retail shop up to the third floor. The upshot, though, was that both Rich Plum and I were suddenly laid off. Within a month Rich tragically jumped

---

[11]Larry Bensky, "Mayor Dianne Feinstein: Historical Essay," FoundSF, http://foundsf.org/index.php?title=Mayor_Dianne_Feinstein.

to his death from Golden Gate Bridge. For a while before the layoff he had been somewhat subdued, but nobody expected this. His closest friends speculated that he had probably been diagnosed with AIDS, and the layoff may have triggered his decision to end his life.

San Francisco General Hospital had set up a special ward for AIDS patients, referred to as Ward 86. For so many at this time, Ward 86 was the last stop. Six months later Ward 5B would be designated as an inpatient unit.

As 1983 ended Ronald Reagan continued to remain silent about AIDS. In December of that year a congressional subcommittee released a report criticizing the U.S. Government for failure to invest sufficient funding in AIDS surveillance and research, but as far as the Reagan administration was concerned, AIDS was a joking matter.

So here I was without a job, getting by on unemployment. But about three months later I got a call from Miss Kitty asking if I would be willing to come back and make some of the ever-popular backpacks Rich had designed. I boldly suggested that what they really needed was a savvy shop manager who knew how to outsource and turn a genuine profit. They agreed to my proposal, and I tackled my new position.

The expanded leather shop took up most of the third floor, leaving a modest workspace and storage area at one side. Applying principals I had learned while working for Nick O'Demus, I immediately set about changing the shop from a hippie-era head shop with some leather to a sophisticated adult leather boutique with a cosmopolitan appeal.

Display cases were arranged around the room along the walls, and the cash register was situated near the stairwell on an antique oak desk. The knee-space of the desk had a small refrigerator for storing poppers. Next to the cash register was a stainless steel bedpan with Ambush match books and small Milk-Bone® dog biscuits. The biscuits were my idea, at first just for fun. But patrons actually liked them because they were excellent breath fresheners, especially after an evening of drinking, smoking, and eating peanuts. They became so popular that they were served up alongside pretzels on the downstairs bar.

I've always been a bit of a practical joker, with a wry, dry sense of humor. I super-glued a dime to the floor near one of the display cases. It was perpetually amusing to see who would bend over and try to pick it up. Another time I arrived at work with a bandage on the side of my forehead. When asked, I explained that I had cut myself shaving. In the afternoon I moved the bandage to the other side of my forehead and waited to see how much time elapsed before someone noticed.

The large flower arrangements for the bar were done weekly by a person known as "Artista" (Dav Fairall), who also did floral displays for Hamburger Mary's and other SOMA businesses. Soft-spoken and somewhat effeminate, usually wearing flowing fabric pants that made him appear to float down the street when he walked, Artista was a truly talented floral designer, but with some decided quirks.

After checking with Miss Kitty I asked Artista if he would

be willing to do a very small arrangement for the leather shop. In particular, I wanted to make a creative display for enema bags, and had mounted one on a wall in front of an antique framed mirror. The bag opening, being quite small, could hold only a couple of stems of roses, tulips, or daisies, and I reckoned it wouldn't be too much trouble for Artista to include something so simple on his shopping list. Artista, however, was disgusted and horrified by the very idea, and thereafter refused to have anything to do with me or the leather shop. Miss Kitty and I laughingly chalked up Artista's reaction to artistic temperament, so I took on the task of getting the rose for the enema bag myself.

The majority of shop income was still the legendary Ambush poppers, which were even mentioned in Randy Shilts' groundbreaking book, *And The Band Played On* (1987). The use of poppers was universal throughout the gay community, and almost all available brands were actually butyl nitrate. But pounding headaches can be just one of the side effects of butyl nitrate. The 'Bush, by contrast, offered genuine amyl nitrate, specially compounded by a local chemist in his basement and delivered to us in ice-cold gallon bottles. This would then be decanted, in house, into 5-dram and 12-dram brown bottles, which were all kept in a special freezer.

On one delivery day the chemist accidentally dropped the big bottle on our stairway and it shattered, spilling amyl nitrate all over the stairwell. The stuff ran down into the bar and seeped into the floor. For days thereafter everyone was light-headed within minutes of entering the bar.

Poppers inhalers were a steady seller. The inhalers were

lidded metal tubes about 2-½ inches long which could be worn around the neck on a beaded chain or a thong. A wick in the tube would be saturated with poppers, making it easy to inhale the vapors on the dance floor or during a sex scene. Logically, we bought wicking, cut it to size, and sold the wicks in packets — I think about 6 or 8 per packet. These were displayed on the checkout desk next to the bedpan filled with matchbooks and dog biscuits.

I can't resist messing with someone if I sense he's at all gullible. One evening there was a young couple in the shop who were clearly rather innocent out-of-towners. They modestly bought a couple of cock rings, and while they were paying, one of them asked about the poppers wicks. I solemnly explained that they were for use in heavy S&M scenes — you put one in each nostril so that you wouldn't bleed so much.

Having been laid off once, I was mindful of one of the owner's admonitions not to make a career of working at the Ambush, so I started thinking about ways to achieve some independence. I was allowed to use the side room as a work space and art studio. In effect I simply took it over. In those days there were no quality whips available for the S&M community, gay or straight. For instance, adult stores and leather shops might offer a whip consisting of a few strips of cowhide latigo stapled or tacked to a thick dowel. I began producing a small selection of well-crafted, braided whips, from light-weight ball whips to a heavy-duty cat-o'-nine-tails. Each was crafted from oak-tanned goat skin leather, which the supplier referred to as "kip." Thinner than cowhide latigo, its flexibility was ideal. Elaborate Turk's-head knots closed the braiding. The most popular of these whips was a hand-beveled, 8-braid, shot-loaded, 4-foot blacksnake whip made from a single kip hide. At the time I didn't realize that I was in the vanguard of the "whip revolution" of the early to mid-80s.

We had some thick rubber cord that had been left over, so that inspired some rubber whip designs as well. One afternoon Tim glued some of the cord into a cock ring. We immediately saw the potential and began making them in three standard sizes. Tim and I filed for a county business license, named ourselves "Mad Dog Enterprises," and began marketing our line of products. We created a mail-order brochure for the whips and began wholesale production for "Jumbo Rubber Cockrings." We looked into the cost of having them mold-manufactured without seams, but at the time we couldn't afford that.

Taking Rich's and Snowflake's advice, I decided to mount an art show consisting of framed calligraphy works and hand-painted one-of-a-kind T-shirts, which I signed "mad dog." To my surprise the show was a modest success. Feeling encouraged, I decided it was time to begin doing more serious works. My immediate inspiration was the work of Paul Cadmus. I carefully studied his cross-hatch drawing style and his works in egg yolk tempera.

Armed with a copy of Cennino Cennini's *Il Libro dell'Arte*, I began preparing panels to paint on. At that time one could get small jars of powdered pigment, distributed by Windsor & Newton. I loved this! I loved the arcane recipes, the work with pigments and binder. I reveled in making my own ink. I happily put plaster of Paris to slake in water for a month to make *gesso sottile*. Our refrigerator at home sported a row of small jars for egg yolk and little batches of color. I also discovered that I had to carefully store egg tempera paintings because cockroaches are ravenous about scrambled eggs on Masonite®.

The Tattoo God, as you can now imagine, was feeling pretty smug. Not only was I becoming an artist, but Tim had begun asking me to design a tattoo for him. I shrugged off this part because I knew that tattoo was a quite different art medium with its own tools and methods. And, I confess, I didn't yet fully appreciate that tattooing is, indeed, Art with a capital *A*.

Late in September, 1984, the first Folsom Street Fair took place. Modeled on the popular Castro Street Fair founded by Harvey Milk and titled "Megahood: the Folsom Street Fair," it was brilliantly conceived as a political organizational tool with an ambitious set of goals: supporting SOMA businesses, raising money for charities, uniting and empowering the diverse South of Market businesses, changing the perception that the South of Market was a blighted area awaiting redevelopment, and fighting for the survival of the SOMA's gay presence in the wake of AIDS.[12]

The timing couldn't have been more ideal, as September is San Francisco's warmest month. From the outset, the fair included a dance stage featuring live bands and musical artists, spaces for local crafts and artists, booths for charities

---

[12]Kathleen Connell and Paul Gabriel, "The Power of Broken Hearts: The Origin and Evolution of the Folsom Street Fair," Folsom Street Fair History, http://www.folsomstreetevents.org/history.

and AIDS education groups, and almost 5 blocks of space for the leather community to revel and be visible to the world as a substantial political force.

The success of the Folsom Street Fair was immediate. It would go on to become an international event, drawing visitors from around the world, and raising hundreds of thousands of dollars for local charities.

As the weeks passed, the horror-stories increased. Men diagnosed with AIDS were being evicted from their apartments, fired from their jobs, and shunned by their families who were nevertheless quick to claim a man's estate when he passed away, even if there was a will in place. The Social Security Administration preferred interviewing patients by phone rather than face-to-face. People were scared — and with good reason. There was still no solid understanding of how AIDS was being transmitted until sometime in 1984. By then more than 6000 cases had been reported in the U.S.

In July of 1984 Jon Sims, who had accomplished so much for LGBT performing arts, succumbed to AIDS, barely 7 months following his diagnosis. More than 1500 people attended his memorial service held at Grace Cathedral.

That year Geoff Mains published *Urban Aboriginals: A Celebration of Leathersexuality*, an astonishingly intimate and pioneering exploration of gay male S&M culture related as a series of stories. His notion of subcultural tribalism would have a lasting impact on the Modern Primitive Movement, which included Fakir Musafar (Roland Loomis) and master piercer Jim Ward, author of *Running The Gauntlet* (2011).

Also in 1984 a waitress in her fifties named Mary Jane Rathbun began volunteering weekly in San Francisco General's Ward 86, wheeling patients to radiology and taking their specimens to the lab. A long-time activist for a variety of causes, she habitually delivered marijuana-laced brownies to patients. Everyone knew her simply as "Brownie Mary." She would go on to become a media sensation, and her efforts brought national attention to the benefits of cannabis on treating the wasting syndrome common in AIDS victims.

In October of that year, under continued pressure from Mayor Dianne Feinstein, SF Public Health Director Mervyn Silverman ordered all San Francisco bathhouses and sex clubs to close immediately. The decision was amazingly short-sighted, because the baths and clubs represented an immense educational resource.

By the end of 1984 there were more than 7,000 cases of AIDS reported in the U.S. Almost 6,000 of those had died, yet President Reagan continued his silence.

As the AIDS deluge grew, so did the hate and fear. In 1985, 13-year old hemophiliac and AIDS patient Ryan White was barred from attending school in Indiana. His case brought additional national attention to HIV/AIDS and helped bring about awareness that AIDS wasn't solely a gay issue, but that it affected everyone.

I Become an Artist

In the fall of 1985 I mounted my third and most ambitious art show at the Ambush — a half dozen egg tempera paintings and numerous drawings focused on the male form. I sold practically everything and pocketed nearly $2,000. For a modest art show in a sleazy South of Market bar in the mid-1980s that was quite a haul.

While the show was still up a Dutchman named Rob Meijer stopped by the leather shop and introduced himself. He was promoting a line of greeting cards produced by the RoB Gallery — his Amsterdam combination art gallery and leather shop. Sporting a mustache and narrow goatee, he looked for all the world as though he might have stepped right out of Rembrandt's painting *Dutch Masters*, but without the wide-brimmed beaver skin hat. He was witty, urbane, and delightful, and we hit it off right away.

I learned that RoB Amsterdam was the premier gay art gallery and leather purveyor in Europe, exclusively representing artists such as Tom of Finland, Nigel Kent, photographer/choreographer Hans van Manen, Keso Dekker, and American expatriate artist Bastille (Frank Weber).

I was therefore astonished when Rob offered me a show at the gallery in Amsterdam. To say I was thrilled would be putting it mildly. I told him that because the present show had virtually sold out, it would take at least a year to generate enough artwork for another show. Rob said that was OK, and he would be returning in a few months.

In July Hollywood acting legend Rock Hudson issued a press release from a Paris hospital announcing that he was dying of AIDS. This was the first time a celebrity had come out as having AIDS. His death followed a short time later, in October, and his passing had an immediate national and international impact on the visibility of AIDS. Just one month previously Dame Elizabeth Taylor, Dr. Michael Gottlieb, and Dr. Mathilde Krim had announced the creation of the American Foundation for AIDS Research.[13]

The Thanksgiving feast that year spanned all three floors of the 'Bush. On the first floor a nude hunk lay on his back on the pool table, practically hidden from view by arrangements of hors d'oeuvres and flowers spread over his body. On the second floor the deli tables sported a wide variety of entrées and side dishes including turkey, cold poached salmon, pulled pork, and all the trimmings. The third-floor leather shop was transformed into the dessert station. And, of course, each floor had the obligatory bowl of acid punch. It was a food orgy of Roman proportions. I loaded up a big plate of food and took it across the street to Animal, who glared at me in his usual manner, but took the offering of food nonetheless.

---

[13] Author unknown, "Thirty Years of HIV/AIDS: Snapshots of an Epidemic," amfAR: Making Aids History, http://www.amfar. org/thirty-years-of-hiv/aids-snapshots-of-an-epidemic/25.

I Become a Tattooer

Like the proverbial squeaky wheel Tim continued to pester me about designing a tattoo for him. Still maintaining that I didn't sufficiently understand the medium, I suggested taking him to see Phil Payton, who by then was working at the "Picture Machine" on Geary Street, owned by Pat Martynuik, a Canadian artist legendary for his speed of execution.

Tim didn't have any particular tattoo concept in mind, other than he wanted one. We chatted a bit with Phil and started browsing the flash on the walls. Roomy and well organized, the Picture Machine had already been in business for over a decade. There was a wealth of flash on the walls, and we spent quite some time looking at the wide variety of images. But this time I really began to look at the images, studying line, composition, and colors. And the more I looked, the more I began to think to myself, "I could do that." I asked Phil if he might be willing to help me learn, and Phil said "yes."

I tackled this new medium in the same way I had tackled the Liszt B-Minor Sonata or egg tempera painting — with enthusiasm and methodical determination. Although Pat wasn't taking on any apprentices right then, Phil agreed to spend time with me during quiet periods at the shop. A proper apprenticeship is the traditional way to learn tattooing, but I wasn't going to let that little detail stop me.

The timing for all this couldn't have been better. From the art shows I had enough money set aside to invest in the tools and equipment I would need. When I told the owners of the Ambush that I wanted to sublet the space next to the leather shop and that I could pay for the additional things I would need myself, they were enthusiastic, because they saw a business advantage to having a tattooer on the premises. So for a very modest $100 per month for rent I not only had a space where I could get going, but a ready-made, budding clientele.

There was some trouble at the Ambush, though. We found out that the owners had inexplicably skipped paying payroll taxes for a number of months. Under threat of being shut down, a deal was reached whereby an official would stop by weekly to collect cash payments for the taxes plus a portion of the resulting fine. At least for the time being, things seemed alright; so I continued with my plan.

At our own expense Tim and I began renovating the side room adjacent to the leather shop. I needed an independent sink with hot running water, so I hired David Backstrom, the in-house handyman. We repainted the walls, improved the lighting, put up mirrors, rebuilt the cabinetry, and mounted a fire extinguisher. There was a niche in the cabinetry that we turned into an art display which also featured a bonsai tree changed out monthly by our friend, "Bonsai" Pete Vafiades. Having experienced annual hospital I.G. inspections when I served as an Army medic in the early 70s, nothing was overlooked — right down to proper electrical outlets.

A vital part of the tattooist's equipment is a working autoclave. Needle groups and stainless steel machine tubes must be bagged, dated, and sterilized. And in order to get a license, the health inspector wants to see both the autoclave and a sample sterilized package.

Because my startup budget was limited I did some looking around and tracked down a used equipment place in Oakland that had a fantastic assortment of everything from industrial-sized kitchen equipment big enough to make a hot tub to strange old motor parts.

There I found a handsome old Pelton & Crane FL2: a solid, heavy chrome marvel from the 1930s or 40s. I think I got it for about $60 because the manager thought the heating elements were burned out. All it actually needed to get it going was a new power cord to replace the old badly-frayed one. I was lucky enough to find a local medical equipment repair guy who had been in business for years and had a garage full of equipment parts. That autoclave was an impressive addition to the studio decor, and I used it for the entire 21 years I tattooed in the City. It was big enough that, as a favor, I autoclaved urethral sounds and other metal sex toys for friends.

Two or three times a week I would head over to the Picture Machine and spend time with Phil. Over the years tattooers had developed their own methods of working with their materials, and they tended to be rather secretive about certain aspects of the craft that they believed made their work better than the competition's.

At the time there was no such thing as pre-made needle groups in individual sterile packs. A tattooer had to know how to solder his own needles together in different configurations, attach them to a short stainless steel rod called a needle bar, and test them for damaged needles by lightly dragging the soldered needles across his thumbnail. If it scratched your thumbnail, that meant one of the needles had a damaged tip and you couldn't use it. A jeweler's loupe helped with this task, but the scratch test was infallible.

Colors arrived in powder form, and tattooers mixed them with their own wetting agent. Although ordinary distilled water was really quite sufficient, tattooers over the years had their own special concoctions which might include Listerine mouthwash, witch hazel, camphor, glycerin, oil of clove (eugenol), isopropyl alcohol, or even vodka for its ethyl alcohol content. By the mid-1990s tattoo supply houses began offering pre-dispersed colors and proprietary wetting solution.

It's important to keep in mind that tattooing began as a folk art, with knowledge handed from person to person. The different home-made wetting solutions certainly would not have been lab-scientific mixtures. Instead, they were more in the class of home-remedy recipes, with an eye to helping ink disperse better, helping ink carry on the needles better, reducing risk of infections, or all of the above.

Some of the colors are very strong, notably dark blues and greens. A little of either of these pigments goes a very long way, and they must be tempered with at least a little white. The darkest blue is so powerful that Phil warned me to take the bottle into the alley to add any wetting agent because if any of the powder got spilled, blue would spread for yards, making it almost impossible to clean up completely.

Tattoo machines are the most important tools of the trade, and learning what makes a machine run smoothly and

efficiently requires patience and experience. A would-be
tattooer must learn from someone in the trade. No manual
can replace being shown hands-on how to keep machines in
good working order. Most tattooers use two machines in a
session, one for outlining and one for filling in, or shading.
An outliner machine may have smaller coils than a shader
machine and is set to run slightly faster in order to lay down
a smooth line in one pass. A shader machine, on the other
hand, runs somewhat slower, and its heavier coils provide
a smooth, steady speed ideal for filling in.

A tattoo machine is a deceptively simple device.
Essentially, it's a metal frame that supports one or two
copper-wound electro-magnetic coils, an armature bar, and
a 2-piece spring connecting the armature bar to the frame.
When direct current is passed to the coils, they become
magnets that pull the armature bar to them, but the motion
breaks the current's path, causing the bar to fall back to its
original position, only to repeat the process. This reciprocal
motion pistons the needle bar, which passes from the top of
the armature bar through a removable tube also supported
by the frame. The tube functions much like a ballpoint
pen barrel — it's what the tattooer grips while running the
machine. The entire range of motion is about ⅛th of an
inch. When the needles are touched to the skin, they drive
pigment particles into the skin.

Tattoo professionals never refer to a tattoo machine as a
"tattoo gun," and some will berate unsuspecting customers
who don't make that distinction, somewhat like the "Don't
call it Frisco" way of thinking. Personally, I believe that
professional nomenclature is meant for professionals.

When you explain that your gums are bleeding or you might need a root canal, your dentist doesn't expect you to say "gingiva" or "endodontia" or "apicoectomy." In fact, he explains things in everyday language. Interestingly, comix and poster-artist-turned-tattooer Greg Irons (1947-1984) seemingly thumbed his nose at the whole notion, because one of his business cards sported the phrase "Have Gun, Will Travel," borrowed from the title of an American Western TV series that aired from 1957 to 1963.

Typically displayed on tattoo parlor walls, tattoo "flash" is a prepared design or group of designs intended to show customers what's available and also for use in rapid tattooing. Prepared designs have long been a staple part of any tattoo establishment, particularly in shops situated near military bases. Having prepared designs on hand meant that a tattooer wouldn't have to draw a fresh design every time he wanted to use it. The customer could choose what he wanted, usually based on how much he was prepared to spend. An artist could modify a flash design or create a custom design on request.

For each design in the displayed flash there was a corresponding pattern transfer that the tattooer could use repeatedly. The old-timers etched these designs onto pieces of celluloid with an awl or a scribe. They then sprinkled the sheet with powdered graphite, thereby filling the inscribed lines, blew off the excess, then carefully placed it onto the skin, which had been coated with enough petroleum jelly for the graphite to adhere. Acetate eventually replaced the highly flammable celluloid.

Tattooers typically traded designs or sold their flash in

sets, and a well-established business could have file cabinets filled with thousands of designs on acetate. I remember seeing such cabinets at the Picture Machine and wishing that I could be allowed to dig around in them because these designs are an intimate record of tattoo design history.

Some people look down on the use of tattoo flash, arguing that while it's fine to use flash for inspiration, tattoos really ought to be custom designed to create a unique and original piece. For working tattooers, though, it's quite common to borrow elements from different designs and rearrange them to suit the needs of the moment.

Custom designs were (and still are) handled a bit differently. I learned how to make a tattoo pattern transfer by tracing the design backward with a particular kind of pencil originally manufactured for use with spirit duplicators — those ditto machines used in virtually every school across the country. After cleansing the skin, the tattooer applied a coat of stick deodorant to the area to be tattooed, which rendered the surface of the skin sticky enough to pick up the purple pencil mark. The pencils gradually disappeared from usage as ditto machines were replaced by modern copy machines, but I had the good fortune to have acquired a box of them, brand name *Mephisto,* from a friend. I continued to use this method when making transfers larger than the limits of a thermal copier.

Tim and I registered the business name *Mad Dog Tattoo* as a DBA of *Mad Dog Enterprises*, then went to register with the health department. The required inspection was anticlimactic. The inspector, who seemed bored and in a hurry, merely glanced around the room, checked for hot running water, and asked to see a sterilized package with the tell-tale dark striping of the sterilizing tape. That was it — none of the rigor of a military I.G. inspection that I was expecting.

Thanks to Phil's recommendation, I was able to order my first supplies from National Tattoo Supply in New Hyde Park, on Long Island, a company that sold only to licensed tattooers who were vouched for by existing customers (in 1991 they moved to Allentown, PA).

I set about soldering up needle groups, packaging, and sterilizing them along with stainless steel tubes. I practiced on oranges. Citrus rind is easy to tattoo but forces accuracy because, like human skin, there is no correcting any line once it has been laid down.

No matter how much one practices, the time finally comes to put metal to skin. Every tattooer is eternally grateful to those who were willing to be the first subjects. Finally, the shop was ready and so was I. In June, 1986, with Phil's guidance, I executed my very first tattoo on my partner Tim, a copy of one on my arm that had been designed by my friend REX. It consisted of two hearts with a lock through them, little blue flowers, and a banner with the phrase *True Love* across the top. My mentor Phil Payton was there to guide me, and I remember being nervous as hell and a little shaky, but I got through it. I was on my way. My own tattoo is now blurry with age, but in my mind's eye it's as fresh as the day it was done. I would never change it or cover it.

On that day, the Tattoo God grinned a big wide grotesque grin and, gleefully dancing around, peed his pants.

Over time I continued Tim's tattoos and would joke that he was my scratch pad.

My first customers were co-workers and patrons of the bar. I didn't charge very much and was willing to accept trades. Gary traded me a Jacob's Ladder made from a neon light transformer that generated a high voltage "climbing arc" display seen in many old Sci-Fi movies. The zzzt-zzzt-zzzt of the arc was quite dramatic. I loved it and put it on display. The piece I did on Gary's forearm was bat wings framing a sinister biker-style skull, all in black. I had overworked the black, and he scabbed up something fierce, but he was happy.

Gary and I had worked together for Nick O'Demus. Formerly an itinerant midwest evangelist preaching from the tailgate of a pickup truck, Gary had transformed into a masochistic hippie biker who loved vintage Airstream trailers, pink plastic flamingos, Harleys, and ball torture. He decided to get rid of the Jacob's Ladder because one evening he straddled it nude, and the electric arc practically knocked him across the room when it hit his balls. That was a little too much — even for him.

Periodically, I would consult with Cliff Raven if I had a question, usually by telephone. Here was a man who really didn't have to give me the time of day, much less advice, but he was consistently gracious and always gave me a relevant tip. While I wished I could go down to Los Angeles and spend some serious time with him, I simply couldn't afford it. I figured that when it came my turn to be helpful to someone just starting out, I owed it to Cliff to be just as generous.

One of Cliff's sayings was "The tattoo isn't finished until the photo is taken." Accordingly, I dutifully took a photo of all my finished pieces with my trusty Polaroid 600. For a time I tried numbering them as well but eventually gave that up.

"Ken" wanted a hummingbird on the right side of his pubic area. This was my first experience tattooing a somewhat private area, and I made every effort to be detached and professional, placing a towel over his privates so that he might feel comfortable with the process. Everything went fine, and I asked him if taking a photo was okay with him. He stood in front of the wall and removed the towel. As soon as I aimed the camera at him he sprung an erection and confessed that being photographed nude was a real turn-on for him, and would I mind giving him one of the photos. I was beginning to see that this tattooing thing was going to be one surprise after another.

My first tribal tattoo, an arm band of alternating narrow black and red flame-like shapes, was on Steve, one of the Ambush bartenders. He was a hefty bear type of guy, and that tattoo seemed to take hours. Because a tattoo machine weighs about a half pound, it would only take about 30 minutes for me to begin feeling pain in the tendons at the base of my thumb (*abductor pollicis longus* and *extensor pollicis brevis*). I would have to stop and give my hand a rest.

Learning to wield a tattoo machine comfortably and confidently takes time. One machine is used for doing line work, and a second machine is used for filling in the colors (shading). Liner machines and shader machines are adjusted a bit differently from each other.

Needle groups are soldered in varying configurations for liners or shaders. Needles in a liner group are clustered tightly together, while needles in a shader group are spread out, not unlike a paint brush. No matter which type is in use, there is always excess ink in the way, which is quite frustrating at first. Furthermore, when you're learning to manipulate a shader into narrow spaces, it feels for all the world like trying to use a shovel to frost a cupcake.

Before the AIDS crisis, tattooers typically worked without gloves. Additionally, used needle groups could be cleaned in an ultrasonic tank and then re-sterilized, to be disposed of only when needles began to get flattened on the side that rubbed against the tube wall. From the outset, however, I always wore latex gloves, and I never used any needle group more than once. Later, when disposable plastic tubes became available, I would count myself among the first to switch from using metal tubes.

One of the people who showed up at the bar now and then was a straight woman tattooist who lived and worked in Phoenix. She was a friend of one of the bartenders. A dominatrix of some sort, she was always dragging around a young man by a leash attached to his collar and would get all snotty about it if anybody made a pass at him. She assured me that I should work up some unicorn tattoo designs, because little unicorn tattoos were very popular in Phoenix, and, by inference, the rest of the world. Reluctantly but dutifully, I drew a couple of small unicorn designs. More than 27 years later, I have yet to tattoo a small unicorn on anyone.

"Jimmy," one of the Ambush regulars, was a sweet,

gentle man who worked for a nearby florist. One evening, over a beer downstairs, we got into a conversation and he began asking questions about tattooing. Then he asked, "How do you practice tattooing?"

With a perfectly straight face, I explained that, for a fee plus a signed recommendation from a working tattooer, you could get a San Francisco County Tattoo Learner's Permit allowing you to practice on unclaimed corpses at the City Morgue. Since the bodies were unclaimed and would be cremated anyway, you could tattoo any part of the body except the face. After successfully completing ten tattoos, you were then automatically licensed to work in a tattoo shop anywhere in the state. I even offered to take him to the morgue and show him the rubber gear and goggles I was required to wear. Poor Jimmy was so concerned about this that he asked his doctor if it was true.

Scott Taylor (Hampton), a good friend of ours, was a porn star famous for being able to insert his pinkie finger all the way into his urethra. Scott had an ongoing fascination with Frankenstein's monster and maintained a considerable collection of Frankenstein-related photos, illustrations, comics, and booklets.

Scott's tattoo idea was unique for the time — random tattoos covering one arm from wrist to shoulder, ending with large tattooed sutures, as though that arm had once belonged to someone else but had been grafted onto Scott. The tattoos at the very top were to look as though they had once extended beyond the suture line. We got started with a couple of pieces, but the project actually spanned 2-3 years because Scott would want time between sessions to think about what to add next.

Working in a bar atmosphere had its drawbacks. Before long, I refused to work on anyone visibly intoxicated or high on drugs. I didn't mind if they wanted to smoke a joint, but that was the limit. Only once did I try to tattoo while stoned on marijuana, and it was an awful experience because I just couldn't stay focused. I vowed that never again would I tattoo while under the influence of anything, figuring that clients were paying me good money to be clear-headed.

That summer, Rob Meijer came by the shop again, and I gave him a tattoo of a devil skull on the middle of his chest. This time he proposed that I come to Amsterdam as a guest tattooist at the RoB Gallery. I was thrilled by the offer, especially after learning that celebrated gay British tattooer and piercer Mr. Sebastian (Alan Oversby) had also been a guest tattooer at the gallery. We made a plan for me to visit in February of the next year because the Amsterdam Tattoo Convention was scheduled for the first part of March.

Failed third-party presidential candidate Lyndon LaRouche and a group of his followers calling themselves PANIC, the Prevent AIDS Now Initiative Committee, spearheaded Proposition 64, a measure to be put on the November California ballot that could have led to a quarantine of persons with HIV. Among their awareness-boosting slogans was "Spread Panic, Not AIDS."

Tim and I, along with our porn-star friend Scott Taylor Hampton, staged a small protest about the quarantine initiative during that year's Up Your Alley fair which took place on Ringold alley, notorious for late-night cruising.

This was the second year for the fair, founded by 1985 IML winner Patrick Toner (thereafter, the fair moved to Folsom Street at Dore alley). We swathed Scott in used canvas drop cloth, somewhat like a mummy, blindfolded him, then used rope to tie him to a chain link fence. We then secured an anti-quarantine banner to the ropes. Mr. Toner was not at all pleased and threatened to call the police if we didn't cease. Thankfully, the proposition was handily defeated. That didn't discourage the Larouchites, however, who reintroduced the measure in 1988. It, too, was defeated.

At the end of that November things at the 'Bush took a catastrophic turn. The old man who had been the landlord passed away, and the property went to a daughter. When her attorneys visited the building, they noted that the two upper floors had been remodeled by the business in violation of zoning requiring that those floors remain residences with separate entries. She sued the Ambush, and the insurance was immediately canceled. On December 6, 1986, guests and employees arrived only to find closed doors with a note announcing that the 'Bush had closed, permanently.

The loss of the Ambush was immense for a lot of people. More than 30 employees were suddenly out of work, including myself. What I had invested in creating a tattoo venue was down the drain. Even worse, a faithful group of regulars suddenly had nowhere to hang out. Sure, there were other South of Market bars, but they simply weren't the same.

Before the internet and all of its impersonal connectedness, gay bars were the original places where you could meet and interact socially with your own kind. Since the early 1950s, gay bars were legally allowed to operate in California, thanks to a 1951 California Supreme Court decision in *Stoumen v. Reilly*. There were still hazards in going to a gay bar, such as police entrapment of men leaving the bars, but by the 1980s gay bars were easy to find, even in smaller towns.

Whether the clientele were leather men, "sweater queens," or regular guys, these were the places you could go to meet up with friends and feel a sense of community, of something shared that made it a little easier to live with the homophobia, the senseless bashings and murders, the feeling of being in a war zone dominated by AIDS.

In that year U.S. Surgeon General C. Everett Koop called for a comprehensive program of sex and AIDS education and urged the widespread use of condoms.

Dedicated to his friend Marvin Feldman, gay rights activist Cleve Jones created the first panel of what would become the AIDS Memorial Quilt.

More than 28,000 cases of AIDS had been reported to date, with more than 24,000 deaths. The death of gay French author Jean Genet in April went virtually unnoticed.

The *Bay Area Reporter* obituaries pages were sad testaments to the passing of friends and loved ones. Nobody wanted to read the obituaries, but we were helplessly drawn to them, knowing also that the printed items represented only some of the deaths happening all around us. By now there were approximately 40 obituaries per month, or just over 10 per week.

And still the Reagan administration remained silent.

At the 1986 centenary rededication of the Statue of Liberty, Bob Hope was on stage entertaining the all-star audience which included the Reagans, who were seated with French President François Mitterand and his wife. During his monologue Hope joked, "I just heard that the Statue of Liberty has AIDS but she doesn't know if she got it from the mouth of the Hudson or the Staten Island Fairy." The Reagans laughed. The Mitterands were aghast.[14]

---

[14]Karen Ocamb, "Ronald Reagan's Real Legacy: Death, Heartache and Silence Over AIDS," The Bilerico Project, http://bilerico. lgbtqnation.com/2011/02/ronald_reagans_real_legacy_death_ heartache_and_sil.php.

ON MY OWN: PART 1

With no income on the immediate horizon, I slogged along on unemployment compensation. Even that had been delayed because of the debacle over the Ambush payroll taxes. In my mind getting to Amsterdam had become vital, and I was willing to go further into debt to get there.

In mid-February I arrived in Amsterdam, where I was met at the airport by Rob, and we proceeded by car toward The RoB Gallery at Weteringschans 273, a half-hour drive of about 22 kilometers into the old-town canal district. Typical of most European cities, there was an exciting blend of the historic and the glaringly modern. Most notable, though, was the widespread graffiti, much more than I had seen in other cities.

Finally, we arrived at the gallery. Because the narrow building served as home, workshop, gallery, and leather retail store, every bit of space was utilized, frequently serving double duty.

On entering, there was the main shop and office where items were elegantly displayed in individual cases. A stairway led down to a basement level that had dungeon equipment displayed for sale, the only full bathroom for the building, plus a nicely-stocked wine cellar. The level above the main store was the kitchen and dining area, and this was where Rob and his partner Dai Evans slept on a large fold-out sofa bed. The next level up was the workshop, where a small crew who arrived every morning manufactured all the leather items for the business. The top level, once an attic, had been converted to a pleasantly modern sunlit guest area which additionally served as storage for artwork not displayed on the floors below.

The first hazard one encounters in old Amsterdam homes are the extremely narrow, nearly vertical staircases. Because houses, especially canal houses, were taxed based on their width, the ever-thrifty Dutch built narrow, tall houses which required crazy-ass stairways. Think of wedges of pie stacked on top of each other, wide ends alternating to create tapering steps barely deep enough to place your toes at the widest part. For the unpracticed, going up the stairs was manageable, but coming down the stairs required serious concentration and total sobriety.

I learned that I would be tattooing in the kitchen area and was introduced to Gaeton, the French houseboy. I got unpacked and set up. That evening, Rob took me to several leather bars, including Argos and the Cuckoo's Nest. At each of the bars we visited, Rob had mounted large posters proclaiming the new tattoo artist at the RoB Gallery. He introduced me to bar owners, bartenders, and customers that he knew well. I started tattooing and making appointments the very next day.

One of my very first clients was a short, handsome British guy in his early 40s, who had been a merchant marine and who sported a colorful assortment of old-style seafaring tattoos that included anchors, mermaids, and nautical stars. He wanted to re-ink lettering on the palms of his hands. On his left hand was tattooed the word "Please," and on his right hand was "Thank You." He explained that on paydays the seamen stood in line before a desk where the paymaster doled out each person's pay. On reaching the desk the seaman was required to hold out his left hand ("Please") and salute with his right hand ("Thank You").

A couple of days after I arrived Rob took me to meet his life-partner Dai Evans, who was in hospital for an HIV-related issue. The hospital was a beautiful structure, with gardens and courtyards where patients and visitors could enjoy each other's company in pleasant surroundings. Dai would be there during most of that visit.

One of the people I met through Rob was Dutch tattooer Henk Schiffmacher, better known in the tattoo world as Hanky Panky. His tattoo shop was also a well-appointed tattoo museum. He was quite gracious, and I had the good fortune to spend some time with him and some of his friends over a beer or two near the shop.

During one of the conversations the chatter came around to types of customers, a perennially favorite topic among tattooers. Henk observed that one could easily spot the gay guys because "they always want something macho."

As a gay American accustomed to homophobic comments, I was at first a bit angry that he would make such a blanket statement. Over time, though, as I gained more experience, I realized that he was right. I also learned that the Dutch can seem oddly brusque at times and wisely concluded that he wasn't being derogatory at all.

One of the difficulties of working in Amsterdam was a lack of ready access to reference materials of any useful sort. While that's a great challenge on one hand, it did mean that for virtually every piece I did, I had to draw it up from scratch, usually out of my head, within a short time frame. I certainly could have benefited from the vast collection of flash I had seen at Pat Martynuik's Picture Machine.

The culminating event of that trip was the 1987 Amsterdam Tattoo Convention, for which Rob had obtained tickets weeks before. It was my first tattoo convention, and I spent hours visiting each booth, taking photos with Rob's camera, and getting to watch some of the top names in the business. It was a humbling experience. Despite all my bravado, I realized I had a long way to go if I wanted my work to be as good as what I was seeing there.

My initial visit was only for a couple of weeks. I had made money, but actually did little more than break even, so Rob and I agreed that subsequent visits would be longer. I made a total of three trips to Amsterdam.

Shortly after arriving back home I attended the March, 1987, National Tattoo Convention in San Diego. The feeling and atmosphere differed noticeably from the Amsterdam convention. There was none of the welcoming inclusiveness I had experienced in The Netherlands.

Gauntlet owner and piercing legend Jim Ward was also at the convention, doing piercings in a nearby motel room, and I decided to get my septum pierced. Jim is a sweet, gentle soul whose calm demeanor immediately puts anyone at ease. Along with the bead ring jewelry he gave me a septum retainer — a small device he had invented for people who, for whatever reason, couldn't always display a highly visible piece of jewelry in their nose. When in place the retainer could be flipped up into the nostrils and thereby be practically invisible.

I say "practically invisible" because, on the return flight from San Diego, a small, elderly lady seated next to me managed to spot it and asked me what it was. I leaned toward her and in a soft voice explained that it was part of an ongoing UCSF Medical Center study into permanent acupuncture to control random rage episodes, and that I had been doing very well for several weeks.

My financial situation was dire. The landlord, who had tolerated late rent payments for a while, was becoming demanding. Reluctantly, I decided to try getting into one of the local tattoo shops. As it happened, Lyle Tuttle was in the process of moving from his famous shop on 7th Street, next to the Greyhound Bus station, to a newly remodeled, state-of-the-art address on Columbus Ave. I made the call, and he agreed to talk to me. Armed with my portfolio of drawings and photos, I went to see him.

Lyle was immediately gracious and showed me around the new shop, pointing out where the artist stations would be. During the nearly hour-long interview he took his time going through my portfolio and asking questions. I told him of my university music training and my service as an Army medic. My sole caveat was that I wanted to be able to go to Amsterdam for one month a year. Interview finished, he said he wanted to talk it over with his wife, and that he would contact me within a couple of days.

When he called I was stunned when he said that he had

decided against taking me on because he was concerned about the "gay thing" and the situation with AIDS. For a long time after I was angry, convinced that Tuttle was just another homophobic asshole. Eventually, though, I conceded that he had every right to be fearful. After all, everyone was fearful, and this was just one manifestation of the generalized panic affecting the entire country. Given that experience, though, I didn't even bother trying to get into another shop.

As the saying goes, "when life hands you roadkill, make Sloppy Joes." I decided to be mobile, going to the customer. I created elaborately-drawn flyers and Tim and I set about putting them on phone and power poles in the Castro and South of Market, on bulletin boards in laundromats and bars, even leaving some on the street alongside other trash.

With an antique doctor's bag and a small, brightly-painted suitcase I had found at a thrift store, I put together a compact, travel-size setup. On arriving at a person's home I would clean off the dining or coffee table and spread out a 13-gallon plastic garbage bag on which machines and inks were set out. At the end of the session it was easy to reach inside the garbage bag, grasp all the leftover materials, and simply turn it inside out. For those clients who were from out of town I had negotiated with a friend to use his house while he was at work.

In March, concerned activists outraged by the government's woefully inadequate response to the AIDS crisis, formed the AIDS Coalition to Unleash Power — ACT UP. Their first demonstration took place on Wall Street to protest the enormous profits of pharmaceutical companies.

Reagan's New Right supporters and the Christian-based Moral Majority had consistently taken the position that gays "are only getting what they deserve." AIDS was trumpeted as "God's wrath on homosexuals" and "nature's revenge on gay men." Finally, in June, six years into the health crisis, Ronald Reagan addressed the issue of AIDS in Washington at the Third International Conference on AIDS. By then more than 36,000 Americans had been diagnosed with AIDS, more than 20,000 had died, and the disease had spread to more than 113 countries.

Also in June, the newly-formed ACT UP joined other activist groups in a demonstration at the White House. In an act that made national headlines police wore rubber gloves while arresting protesters.

Meanwhile, back to my story . . .

I was asked if I would publicly put a "Property Of _____" tattoo on the new partner of a couple who wanted to throw a "commitment party" at the Brig, a bar on Folsom Street (now the Powerhouse). I agreed, figuring that it would give me some publicity. I set up in an area that was supposed to be at least somewhat protected from patrons and guests, but that didn't help much. People would come up to congratulate my client and in the process would pat him, hug him, or otherwise make him move. It was hard to concentrate with that going on, along with the shouting and typical bar noise.

That's also when I started becoming aware of the Tattoo God's Universal Tattoo Truths.

The Tattoo God's Universal Tattoo Truth #1:

Inevitably, "Property Of" tattoos and names of boyfriends or girlfriends are a jinx, and a breakup will likely be only a matter of time.

That couple's relationship tanked within three months. It's far better for a couple to pick something symbolic for them — whether it's a butterfly or a beer label doesn't matter — at least it won't need to get covered over down the road.

"Hans" was in town for a few days from Germany. He asked that I meet him for lunch in the Castro district so that he could describe his tattoo idea. When I met him at the restaurant he was wearing a long-sleeved shirt buttoned completely at the neck and wrists, despite the warm temperature. I didn't think much about it at the time.

He wanted a bull's head on each side of his chest such that each nipple ring would also be the bull's nose ring. There was to be a yoke connecting them, and a chain extending from the yoke down his chest and belly to a tattooed cockring. OK, no problem — that is, until he arrived for his appointment and removed his shirt. He had numerous purplish Kaposi's Sarcoma lesions. In the 1980s, Kaposi's Sarcoma was widely known as one of the defining AIDS illnesses, thought to be spread by saliva, as in French kissing, or from using saliva as a sex lubricant.

There were lesions along the area to be tattooed, and I was at a loss as to whether to proceed. He told me that it would be fine with him if I worked around the lesions. I suppose I should have declined to work on him, but at the

same time I knew that he came to me as a last hope. I just
didn't have the heart to say no, particularly since, as far as I
knew, there probably wouldn't be an adverse effect.

While I was working on him I would cross areas that
I was pretty certain might be incipient, as yet uncolored,
lesions. At these spots, his skin felt different under the
needle, as though the skin itself would at any moment
shred like a wet paper towel. On a few other occasions after
that I was certain I could detect Kaposi's Sarcoma on clients
who didn't present with any lesions, simply from that same
feel while tattooing them. Of course, I didn't say anything
because I'm not a medical professional, and I wouldn't want
to change somebody's world based on a layman's hunch.

Later, by the mid-1990s or thereabouts, Kaposi's Sarcoma
didn't seem such a part of the manifestation of AIDS.
Mysteriously, it seemed to disappear from most persons
living with AIDS, although not entirely. Younger people
have no idea what it looked like, and no comprehension of
how much it terrorized the gay community and stigmatized
those who had it, frequently making them a kind of pariah,
cruelly unwelcome or shunned at bars, restaurants, and
public gatherings.

Now and then I would get some business from a straight
person. One such client was a young Latina who wanted a
small decorative piece on her ankle. When I arrived at her
apartment I was greeted by her boyfriend. The boyfriend
wasn't particularly friendly and seemed suspicious of me,
as though I might try to put the make on her.

I was recovering from a cold and still had a slight cough.

While I was working on her foot I had to cough, and because I was wearing gloves, I turned away from her and put my face toward my armpit so that I wouldn't cough or sneeze on our work. Boyfriend immediately bridled and asked, "What's the matter? Do you think her feet smell bad?" I explained my action, and he settled down somewhat, but he continued to give me the stink-eye for the remainder of our session.

For some time I had recommended Noxzema Cream for tattoo aftercare because that had been Cliff Raven's recommendation. Actually, it's pretty good stuff. I had done a tattoo on a young man's chest and went through his care procedure as I bandaged him. A couple of days later he called to announce that he had a bad infection, so I drove over to his home. When I examined the work I was relieved to see that it wasn't actually infected, but it definitely looked irritated and raised up like a large welt. When I asked him what he had been doing, he told me that he had followed instructions carefully, then said, "but, you know, whenever I've used Noxzema before I always get an awful rash." What on earth do you say to something like that? There is a Kashmiri proverb, "giving advice to a stupid man is like giving salt to a squirrel."

The Tattoo God's Universal Tattoo Truth #2:

Tattoo clients hear care instructions in a foreign language.

"Jamie" was a slender, handsome dirty-blonde hustler — an "escort" if you want to be polite. His lanky frame, equally lanky Southern drawl, and downright friendliness just seemed to go right along with an endowment that practically guaranteed he would never have to buy his own dinner. He was an outspoken vegan who didn't drink or smoke and who had a passionate interest in the Pre-Raphaelite artists.

He came to me with an idea for a Mayan-themed design for the top of his right hip, curving from his pubic area down the outside of his leg to just above the knee. When I arrived at his apartment I was mildly curious about his preparations. He had a variety of fruit and vegetable juices set out in a particular order, along with a glass oral thermometer and a small bottle of Valerian, an herbal extract. Taken orally, Valerian has long been used to induce healthful sleep and relaxation.

As we got started he would dip the thermometer into the bottle of Valerian, then slide the wetted thermometer into his urethra and slowly move it in and out for a few minutes before re-wetting the thermometer. He assured me that doing this helped him stay calm and focused. It must have worked, because he was quite calm through the entire session. All I could think about, however, was how bad things would be if the thermometer ever broke while he was doing that.

There's no kinky quite like British kinky. Maybe it's the accent. "Geoffrey" wanted the head of his penis tattooed purple because he got turned on by guys whose penile glans appears purplish when their penis is erect. This sometimes seems more pronounced in those with very fair skin, and even more pronounced if the person is wearing a cock ring or similar constrictive toy.

A man's dog is actually his second-best friend. Fortunately, his real best friend doesn't bark or sneeze, and I suppose we should all be grateful for that. In spite of its best-pal status, it seems to have a mind of its own, and its demands for attention often lead to trouble. It is heartless, selfish, and greedy, but we coddle it, protect it, flaunt it, joke about it, use it to exert power over others, and are generally unwilling to live without it. In courts of law we swear by the package and refer to it when hurling epithets at those we dislike.

I've never had an issue with tattooing male or female genitalia. As far as I'm concerned it's simply another part of the body, and I have never tacked on a punitive "handling fee." It's my opinion that tattooers and piercers are in the business of working on people's bodies and that genitals simply go with the territory. If there's a problem, it's the practitioner who has the problem.

A common question is "Does a penis have to be erect in order to be tattooed?" The answer is no. In fact, a flaccid penis is much easier to tattoo. Tattooing anyone's genitals is definitely work, though. Logistically, it's awkward. Ideally, you need at least three hands for tattooing penises, scrotums, or labia — one to tattoo with, one to hold and stretch the skin, and another one to wipe away excess ink and blood. For tattooing penises and scrotums I found that using a cardboard toilet paper tube covered with plastic wrap was an excellent prop for stretching the skin. Frequently, I would direct the client to put on gloves and manage the wiping when asked. This participation tactic not only helps the tattooer, it actually helps keep the client focused away from the intense sensations.

We spent quite a bit of time mixing the precise shade of purple that Geoffrey wanted, and I started at the corona of the glans, where it meets the penile shaft. That was the most sensitive for him, and I had to work in brief 10-15 second increments. Also, the wrapped cardboard tube wasn't very helpful here. Once we got over the corona and onto the sloping part of the glans, it was a bit easier going for him, but not much. The glans is quite spongy and it bleeds readily, so I kept Geoffrey busy with the wiping. But as we approached the urethral opening — the piss slit — he said that, surprisingly, it felt really good, and his penis was clearly in agreement as it rapidly gained full erection.

When we were finished Geoffrey mentioned that he had a castration fantasy, but I said I wasn't able or willing to help him with that.

Sometimes a person will remain erect during a genital tattoo. My very first penis tattoo was on "Harry," a young bartender who worked at the Brig (now the Powerhouse). He wanted a snake along the length of his shaft. While I was working, he suddenly ejaculated. When I resumed work his penis was too sensitive to continue, so I agreed to a second session. Based on that experience, I thereafter warned clients that if they thought they might cum, they had better hold off because we would continue no matter what — no second sessions.

For the first couple of years I meticulously worked up each drawing, plotting out lines, colors, and shading. Later on, my drawings became more sketchy, reduced to the basics.

I have always tended to trust people, to take them at their word. I was contacted by a guy who lived in another state. After describing his idea over the phone he asked if I could send him the drawing for his approval, so I naively sent him a completed drawing. When I called him to set up an appointment, he told me he had taken the drawing to a local artist instead. That was the last time I ever gave a client any drawings for any reason.

The Tattoo God's Universal Tattoo Truth #3:

Your tattoo designs, no matter how simple, are worth money. Hang onto them.

I don't recall when, precisely, that I decided to get tested for HIV. Tim had already tested positive some months earlier, so I assumed that I, too, would be positive. At that time an HIV test required mandatory counseling before receiving the results. I did the test and then had to wait a few days for results. At the counseling session I was dumbfounded when I was told that I was HIV negative, and I asked if there could be some mistake. The counselor told me that no, there was no mistake, and that it wasn't at all uncommon for one partner to test positive and the other to be negative. To this day I'm still HIV-negative.

People's reactions to pain are almost as varied as people themselves. For the most part tattooing is a bit like being incessantly chewed by a small bug. In other words, it's annoying but reasonably tolerable. The more sensitive areas are anywhere over a bone, and fleshy parts like the underside of the arm or inside of the upper leg. Most people can deal with the aggravation for 2-3 hours, after which sensitivity magnifies. For first-timers apprehension about possible pain is almost worse than the sensation itself.

Some people remain calm throughout the tattoo session, and it's not uncommon for an experienced tattoo client to doze off during longer sessions. Other people, however, will tense up, hiss, moan, or even worse, jerk without warning. With these people I learned early on to be firm and tell them to shut up and hold still.

I recall one woman who wanted a small butterfly on her thigh. During the consultation she expressed considerable concern about how painful it might be. I honestly never know what to tell people, but I tried to be as soothing as possible. She made an appointment for a few days later. Every day, however, she would call and ask yet again about the pain factor. I tried to be patient, but finally, exasperated, I told her that she should expect something between PMS and childbirth.

One young man was getting a piece on his left arm. I arrived at his apartment and got set up, but he said we would have to wait for a dentist friend to bring some anesthetic. After a long wait the dentist finally arrived and proceeded to inject the client's arm in a number of places. This not only caused the skin to raise up like an angry welt, but it became tough to the touch. It felt like trying to tattoo a football.

Most dental anesthetics contain epinephrine. One of the effects of epinephrine is vasoconstriction — a narrowing of the blood vessels in the vicinity of the injection. Practically speaking, this aids in prolonging the effect of the anesthetic. But one of the drawbacks is that an anesthetic with epinephrine should not be used on extremities like ears, toes, or fingers, as this can potentially lead to gangrene.

Initially, "Bruce" wanted a tattoo on his arm. When we finished, he decided that he also wanted a crescent tattooed across the head of his penis. I had barely started when he had me stop because it was too intense for him. A few months later he returned to have the crescent completed. He had with him a syringe and a couple vials of dental anesthetic that he had found in the trash behind a dental office. When he asked me to inject his penis, I said no and told him of the possible hazard.

Taking no heed, he injected his penis himself — not once, but twice. The injection sites looked a bit like very small eyes. In about fifteen minutes he announced he was numb. His poor willy had withdrawn like a turtle into its shell, and I had to literally pull it from his body. We did the tattoo, and he did heal fine with no adverse effects.

Sometimes a client can really be a royal pain, and that was the case with a young man who was visiting from Australia. He wanted two modest tribal pieces: one on his left bicep, and a complementary one on his pubic area. Placing the transfer on his arm was a serious exercise in patience. He would look at the placement, pronounce it good, and then as soon as I removed the transfer paper, he would ask me to move it a slight bit one way or another. After a few of these exchanges, I was ready to strangle the little twit!

Finally, though, we got through that one, only to repeat

the picky placement game for his pubic area. I got about two inches into the line work when he suddenly begged me to stop, announcing that he just couldn't stand the pain. I talked him into making the line into a small lightning bolt. I have seldom been so glad to be done with someone.

You never know who is taking what kind of medications, or whether or not they've been taking them as prescribed. I was working on a client at his home in Bernal Heights while his partner was reading a magazine in the adjacent room. Suddenly, my client sat upright, staring into space. He started to say something but then slumped, sliding to the floor like a strand of spaghetti slides off a spoon. Thanks to my Army medic training, I realized that he was in the throes of an epileptic seizure, so I rolled him to his side with his head tilted slightly back. I yelled for the partner, but the guy just keep reading, saying, "Oh, don't worry about it — he does that all the time."

October of 1987 was the Second National March on Washington for Lesbian and Gay Rights. The demands this time, which included an end to racism in America and an end to apartheid in South Africa, were broad in scope on the basis that oppression of one group affects oppression of all groups. Featured speakers included Cesar Chavez, Whoopie Goldberg, and Jesse Jackson. Police estimates put the numbers at the actual march to almost half a million.

Also in 1987, North Carolina Republican Senator Jesse Helms added an amendment to the Supplemental Appropriations Act, which directed the president to use executive authority to add HIV infection to the list of excludable diseases which prevent both travel and immigration to the United States. The action was opposed by the U.S. Public Health Service.

ON MY OWN: PART 2

I don't recall who introduced me to the T&P Group, an informal social club in Los Angeles for tattooed and pierced men originally organized in the '70s by Doug Malloy and Jim Ward. Monthly meetings consisted of a potluck dinner, usually followed by piercing sessions.

I was invited to attend a couple of these events, so I went prepared to do tattooing, and I stayed at the home of a friend who lived in the Hollywood Hills. On both occasions I didn't do any tattooing and felt I had pretty much wasted my time. The bright side was that I believed I was at least getting in some self-promotion.

An incident at one of these gatherings had a long-lasting effect on me. "Roger," a young man in his mid-twenties, showed me a large black-and-gray back piece that had been done by Cliff Raven. Good black-and-gray work is similar to a good pencil drawing or sumi painting. Thinning black ink with water allows for delicate shading in ways that don't work as well with colors, both in terms of technique and in the overall effect. Tattoo color schemes, on the other hand, are usually bold, relying more on color contrast over subtlety of shading.

Roger told me that he had later asked Cliff to do a piece in color on his calf, but that Cliff had refused for two reasons: (1) people seeing the color work would tend to ask when he planned to "finish" the black-and-gray piece, and (2) Cliff felt Roger was too young to be adding more significant work and that he should wait until he was in his 30s. I have never forgotten those two admonitions.

More remarkable to me was the notion that it was better for someone to wait for a while before jumping into full-scale body coverage, and, by inference, a degree of maturity would be important in shaping a person's tattoo choices. If Roger had been older, I believe Cliff would have had no problem continuing to work on him, give or take a discussion about black and gray versus color.

The other remarkable thing to me was that Cliff turned down what amounted to a fair chunk of money, and that ethical considerations were more important to him. For me this evolved into three simple rules:

1. Don't hesitate to tell someone they're too young for something, even though chances are they won't see it that way. A highly visible tattoo affects one's opportunities in the job market, especially for young women. Sometimes it's a matter of smart placement.

2. Don't do work that you know will become blurry in a few short years — small lettering, small busy things like fussy, tight Celtic knotwork, etc.

3. To do a tattoo with a hateful or negative message is to participate in that person's world view, or karma, or whatever you want to call it.

A client had come to me to cover or repair a "born to lose" tattoo. I don't understand why someone would want to carry something like that on his body, every day reminding himself that he is somehow unworthy of even the basics of human dignity. I was able to talk him into a revision: "born to lose, live to win."

During most of the 1980s magazines and periodicals featuring tattoos were limited to the biker publications *Outlaw Biker* and *Easyrider*. As such, the tattoos consisted of typical biker themes — skulls, demons, naked ladies, and Harley Davidson wings, done in mostly black and gray.

In the late 1980s, *Easyrider* began publishing *Tattoo*, and *Outlaw Biker* began publishing *Tattoo Revue*, but at first there wasn't any serious qualitative difference from what they had already been publishing.

Gradually, though, one began seeing a wider acknowledgment of tattoo as an art form. Even though tattooing was far more advanced than what was being shown in these magazines, they were initially what the mainstream public saw on the store racks. But a magazine industry shift was beginning which would immensely help shape public perception of tattoo as a true art form.

The best-known of these efforts was *Tattootime*, published by famed tattoo artist Don Ed Hardy. Starting in 1982 with *New Tribalism*, there were only five issues. Even now, years after being out of print, the articles and pictures are as informative and relevant as they were through the 1980s.

Another beautiful but brief effort was Shotsie Gorman's *Tattoo Advocate Journal*. Volume 1 (Spring, 1988) was sumptuous in its formatting and photography, while the intelligent and insightful articles and interviews raised the intellectual bar for other tattoo periodicals of the time.

The mid-1980s was a period of intense interest in not only tattooing, but other forms of body modification. Tattoos were hardly mainstream yet, and body piercing and scarification were even more deeply underground. Those people interested in reclaiming their own bodies for sensual, aesthetic, or sacred purposes were scattered here and there, with few pre-internet methods available for meeting like-minded souls.

The 1989 publication of *Modern Primitives*, edited by V. Vale and Andrea Juno, was a milestone (Re/Search publications, #12). The interviews, stories, and photos brought extreme body modification to a wide audience, and for many it has been a must-have resource for knowledge about body arts.

My flyer campaign was working, business was growing, and my second trip to Amsterdam was considerably more successful, at least in terms of name recognition if not actual revenue. That was the most pleasurable of my three trips. Both Rob and his lover Dai Evans were feeling pretty good, and our friendship grew.

The only memorable bit of awkwardness came as a result of my desire not to be any kind of trouble or nuisance to them. They had given me a key to the building so that I could come and go as I pleased. If I stayed out past their bedtime I quietly let myself in and tiptoed up the stairs in the dark to the top floor where I had my room. But there were a few stairs that squeaked loudly, so earnestly believing that I was doing them a favor, I used soap to stop the squeaking. Dai actually was upset because they were accustomed to using the squeak to gauge who was moving around in the building.

In May-June, 1988, the CDC mailed a brochure to every household in the U.S. titled *Understanding AIDS*. It included information on how AIDS is and is not transmitted and how people can rationally protect themselves. There was also a hotline available for those who had questions.

In November, 1988, Republican Vice-President George Herbert Walker Bush successfully defeated Democratic opponent Michael Dukakis to become the 41st President of the United States.

Business for me really jumped thanks to my friend REX, who did an interview of me for *Drummer* Magazine titled "Prick the Skin," putting me in an international spotlight (#112 [1988], p.39).

I was honored and flattered to be sought out by people in the gay leather community whom I respected. One of these was my long-time friend Mark I. Chester, author and radical sex photographer. I did a small tribal piece on his arm. Later on, I would become one his photography subjects, tattooing for his camera.

I felt equally honored when noted gay playwright Robert Chesley asked me to put a rather lengthy quote from Lawrence Sterne's *Tristram Shandy* on his back: "For all this, I reverence truth as much as any body; and when it has slipped us, if a man will but take me by the hand, and go quietly and search for it, as for a thing we have both lost, and can neither of us do well without, I'll go to the world's end with him. But I hate disputes."

Robert was already spotted with Kaposi's Sarcoma lesions, reminding me of leopard spots, and I worked tenderly and carefully on him. I didn't ask for money. Instead, I asked for copies of his plays, which I later donated to an archive.

One of my most highly visible tattoos was a big tribal dragon on the arm of a handsome Texas boy named Coulter ("Colt") Thomas, who had won the 1983 International Mister Leather title in Chicago and who was very active in the leather community. It had required several sessions at his home on Cumberland Street, near the Dolores Park playground. I recall being nervous whenever I rang the doorbell because his pet Rottweiler always got to the door first, and I was convinced it would tear me to shreds.

"Blair" came to me to start up a piece for his entire back, extending from his neck and shoulders down onto his buttocks. It was my largest tribal tattoo up to that point. I took careful measurements, invested in a roll of tracing paper, and came up with a clean, bold symmetrical design that could be accomplished in sections. With sessions every other week, it took almost three months to finish the piece.

When I set out to put the final segment on his back, between his shoulder blades, I couldn't get the transfer to seat evenly between the other sections. When I asked Blair to stand straight, he told me he had fallen from a cliff as a teen, breaking his back, and it hadn't healed in a straight line. I moved the section up as far as I could to make the discrepancy less noticeable, and we did it. The difference wasn't actually all that noticeable, thankfully. That tattoo got a good deal of local attention, bringing me more business, especially for tribal tattoos.

On October 17, 1989, a few minutes before Game 3 of the 1989 World Series was scheduled to begin at Candlestick Park, an earthquake measuring 6.9 on the Richter scale struck along the San Andreas Fault near Loma Prieta Peak in the Santa Cruz mountains, approximately 70 miles (113 km) south of San Francisco.

At the moment of the quake I was consulting with a would-be client at his home on upper Castro. Because it was built on a rather steep slope, one entered the house on the second level. While we were talking, his collection of kachina dolls suddenly flew off the shelves at us, as though they had come to life and were bent on some kind of revenge. As the house shook, dishes tumbled out of his kitchen cabinets. The house continued to sway after the jolting stopped, making the trees appear to be bobbing. Maybe he felt the earthquake was a bad omen or something because he never got a tattoo from me.

Tim was at work, so I made my way from the Castro to Snowflake's apartment in the Mission District. He had experienced no damage, so we went up onto his roof where we could see most of the city skyline. As the sun was setting, I started walking home and was surprised at how dark everything was. There were no working street lights or street lamps. Drivers were, for a change, extra cautious. When I got home, only one item had been dislodged from its shelf. With all the power out, the only available news was from a transistor radio belonging to the next-door neighbor.

The Loma Prieta quake severely damaged many of the

city's freeways, including the Embarcadero Freeway and the Central Freeway. The quake also caused extensive damage in the Marina District and the South of Market neighborhoods. Despite the significant destruction the earthquake had caused throughout the greater Bay Area, only 67 people died.

It was around the same time that our friend Snowflake, in his typically pragmatic manner, confided that he had been diagnosed with AIDS. He didn't talk much about it, nor would I press him for details, but of course the diagnosis deepened our friendship.

Cultural events and social icons have always influenced tattoo themes. For the historian these design nuggets are a tremendous aid in determining when a tattoo might have been done. During both World Wars, there was the "Rose of No Man's Land" (also "Angel of No Man's Land"), a portrait-style image of a Red Cross field nurse, combined with a rose, that was a tribute to those brave women who attended the wounded and dying in the trenches. Through the 1970s, the logo from Zig Zag Man cigarette rolling papers and artist Art Crumb's Keep On Truckin' character encapsulated the hippie anti-war, free-love, and marijuana culture.

The 1989 movie *Batman* starred Michael Keaton as Batman and Jack Nicholson as The Joker. For the next couple of years Joker and crazed clown images flooded the social conscience and the biker tattoo magazines. At around the same time the Tasmanian Devil, an animated character from Warner Brothers studios, was the subject of a television cartoon series "Taz-Mania." Just like the Joker, Tasmanian

Devil tattoos enjoyed a degree of popularity.

In this business, there's always a surprise customer. "Alain" was a convincing Cher impersonator who wanted copies of Cher's tattoos, particularly those that were visible in magazines like *Vanity Fair*. We didn't do all of them, but over a series of appointments I learned a great deal about the world of impersonators, cross-dressers, and drag. Over the years Cher removed or added tattoos in a steady ebb and flow. I don't know if Alain tried to keep up with the changes.

My third and final trip to Amsterdam was miserable in several ways. This time Rob was very ill but not in the hospital. Dai's illness had also worsened, but he was taking care of Rob at home, who was ensconced in the kitchen-dining area where they usually slept at night and where I tattooed during the day. Trying to work on someone in the same room with Rob was both awkward and at times embarrassing, because Rob was querulous and demanded a degree of quiet that I couldn't always accommodate.

I was wiring money to Tim, but again this would be a trip in which I barely broke even. A nail was coming up through the heel of the engineer boots that I had been wearing almost daily for more than six years. Walking around with that nail poking into my foot created an indented callous, making me think of penitents enduring self-inflicted punishments.

On my return, after nearly five weeks in Amsterdam, I spent an additional two weeks tattooing in New Orleans at Second Skin Leather, located in the French Quarter. The owner, Jay Borne, was a marvel of Southern hospitality, but

I found myself growing weary of strange beds and living out of a suitcase. The seven-week trip was exhausting and saddening. I vowed that never again would I travel to tattoo for such an extended period of time.

In April, 1990, Rob passed away, and Dai followed soon after.

That same month also saw the death of Ryan White, an Indiana teenager who had contracted AIDS through a tainted hemophilia treatment. After being barred from attending school because of his HIV-positive status, Ryan White and his mother became well-known activists for AIDS research and anti-discrimination.

JUNIPER STREET

After nearly three years of making house calls I was busy enough that continuing to work this way was becoming a burden financially. Travel time to and from clients' homes was using what could have been ink time. I was on the lookout for an available shop or space where I could set up with some permanence.

One of my all-time favorite clients was piercing guru and genius Jim Ward, owner of the Gauntlet in Los Angeles. It was Jim who pierced my septum and it was Jim who had given me my Prince Albert. He had moved to San Francisco in order to be with his new partner/master Drew Nicholas, and they occupied a flat on Landers Street, not far from Castro Street.

Jim and Drew had agreed that a portrait of the pagan forest god Cernunnos would be done on Jim's pubic area. I agonized over the drawing, wanting it to be perfect — the face, the antlers and the oak leaves. The work required more than one session, so each time I arrived at the building and rang the bell I had to wait for them to drop the front door entry key from the third floor by a string, because although the doorbell worked, they had no way to buzz someone in.

They confided to me that they were negotiating a lease deal for the top floor of a building at Castro and Market, and we began tossing around the idea of me coming in as the resident tattooer. As badly as I wanted to be grounded in a space, and while I was honored that they felt I would be an asset, I finally decided against the deal. For one thing, I wasn't certain I could successfully meet my portion of the lease (it turns out I easily could have, but I didn't know that). For another, Mad Dog Tattoo wouldn't be a destination — it would be the Gauntlet with a resident tattooer. Lastly, I valued their friendship far more than the business opportunity and never wanted a situation where unforeseen business disagreements could potentially ruin that, or any, friendship.

The new owner of A Taste of Leather asked if I wanted to set up in the back of the shop, which had since moved from Folsom Street to a different, smaller location. But by then A Taste of Leather had become a rather seedy, depressing shadow of what it had once been. I had already learned my lesson about subletting, and once again Mad Dog Tattoo would not be a distinct destination.

A seemingly better opportunity presented itself when the owner of the set of buildings at the corner of 18th and Castro announced that a few business spaces were available, having been renovated following a 1988 fire, which had destroyed the famous Elephant Walk Bar. Located on the second floor, it was an ideal space at an ideal monthly rent of $500. However, the owner refused to lease to a tattoo shop because he didn't want "that kind of riffraff" in his building. I explained that my clients included doctors and lawyers and business professionals, but he was adamant.

In the long run I was relieved that it didn't work out because of the way he treated other tenants; for instance, he wanted the Elephant Walk Bar for himself; but when the business owner wouldn't sell, he tripled the rent, forcing the Elephant Walk out of business.

A friend happened to tell us of a unique living space a short distance from where we were currently living, available at a quite reasonable rent. Located near the end of a dead-end alley off of Folsom Street between 10th and 11th, it had been the carriage house for a pre-1906 earthquake Victorian home that had since been converted to three units.

It was situated at the back of the property, and to get to it, one entered a door at the street next to the front building, passed through what had once been a driveway, then crossed a small courtyard. The upstairs, formerly the hayloft, was a quaint one-bedroom cottage apartment with slanted ceilings and old skylights in both the kitchen and the bath. The downstairs, with its own entry, was an empty space that had been used for storage.

At first it didn't seem to be that much of an advantage. Then I recalled that this part of South of Market had been zoned for artist live-work spaces, and it dawned on me that this could be ideal. Tim and I had lived in a cramped two-room studio apartment for nearly 7 years. We desperately needed more comfortable living quarters, and I desperately needed a permanent work place.

The landlady, a middle-aged hippie living in Berkeley, was at first uncertain about the prospect of renting to a tattoo artist, but I promised her that there would be no street signs, no drop-in foot traffic, and no business conducted in the evenings. For a modest $650 monthly rent we now not only had a workable living space in the heart of the SOMA, but I finally had my own studio. We moved in August, 1990, and would be in that space for the next seventeen years.

We set about painting upstairs and downstairs. The studio required a good deal more work, but with the help of my artist friend Snowflake — a professional interior house painter — we painted the walls, the ceiling with all its beams, and the concrete floor. In exchange for tattoo work, one friend put in fluorescent lighting and another installed a sink with a counter large enough for the autoclave and an ultrasonic tank. Because of the old plumbing the studio sink had to be quite high up the wall, requiring that I stand on a step stool to use it. Whenever clients asked why the sink was so high, I had a ready answer: "so people won't pee in it."

Once we had it fixed up, the studio was a wonderful place to work. Bookshelves held all of my ample collection of art and reference books. There was a 4-drawer file cabinet for drawings, flash, and other files. The drawers were labeled Eenie, Meenie, Miny, Mo, which often amused clients. There was art on the walls, and classical music from the radio. It was a peaceful place.

The location put us practically in the middle of the annual Folsom Street Fair, which extended from 12th Street all the way to 7th Street. By now, September into October had become my busiest time of the year, tattooing locals and visitors who wanted to be sporting new ink for the fair or who wanted to wait until just after the fair to get their work done so that they wouldn't be in a healing state during the festivities.

The courtyard wasn't used much by the tenants of the front building, so we set out cymbidiums and herbs in pots. The south wall received bright light but never much direct sunlight, and we started a collection of smaller cool-growing species orchids — mostly *masdevallias* and *draculas*, but also *odontoglossums, epidendrums, laelias,* and other genera. We mounted them on cork or tree-fern slabs and hung them along the wall. Over time the orchid wall became a stunning display of color, enchanting everyone who came through the courtyard.

Because we were so removed from the street, one of the things we noticed right away was the relative quiet, a most welcome change from the urban noise we had been so long accustomed to enduring.

As evening approached, I would set up the charcoal grill, pour a glass of wine, light a joint, and begin preparing dinner. After years of stove-top meals and no working oven, grilled foods were a treat beyond compare. Grilling became my new hobby, and I was enthralled with being a Patio Daddy-O.

In the peacefulness of the very early morning, before commuter traffic got underway, I would stand out on the little landing in front of our door, smoke a cigarette, and listen to a pair of distant foghorns that we named "Booper" and "Beeper." Booper's slow, languid bass notes contrasted with Beeper's plaintive tenor. The notes from either were spaced at seemingly random intervals, giving one the impression of an intimate, gentle conversation, like long-time lovers cooing in the misty fog.

As Snowflake's health deteriorated, he methodically made preparations, including asking his closest friends which of his belongings they might want after his passing.

I thought quite a while about that and finally told him that I would be happy with his antique table-top hand-operated sewing machine, one that had belonged to his mother.

During the 1990s some things were easing up for gays.

Active for only a few years, the direct-action group Queer Nation was formed in March, 1990. The group was criticized for its confrontational tactics, especially the practice of outing — a public disclosure of a person's sexual orientation.

In August, 1990, Congress passed the Ryan White CARE Act, in spite of considerable opposition by North Carolina Senator Jesse Helms. Ryan, a hemophiliac teenager who became infected with HIV from a contaminated blood treatment, made nation-wide headlines when he was expelled from school because of his HIV status.

In October, 1990, the U.S. Congress repealed a law prohibiting gays from being admitted into the country. Sexual orientation discrimination in the private sector was banned in several states: Colorado (1990), followed by Minnesota and Connecticut (1991).

San Francisco City and County voters finally adopted the Domestic Partners Ordinance known as Proposition K on November 6, 1990. The ordinance recognized non-marriage committed relationships, including those of lesbians and gay men.

On November 26, Congress enacted the Immigration Act of 1990, which, among other stipulations, withdrew homosexuality as a reason for immigration exclusion.

THE MACHO THING

Cultural events and social icons influence our choices of tattoo themes and concepts. Any tattooer who has been at it for a while is innately aware of this. When people choose a tattoo, they do so for two primary reasons. On one hand, they are ostensibly choosing something for or about themselves. But they are also speaking to others around them.

We use cultural tribalism to establish ourselves within a social context or to reflect strong ethnic or cultural identities. We put forth signals, often in the form of symbols, that we are, or want to be, part of a group or a subgroup, and we do not put out signals that are contrary to the group(s) with which we choose to be associated. This is evident in everything from our choices in clothing and automobiles to our choice of tattoos. You're not likely to meet a Latino with a Confederate flag tattoo or a cowboy with a tattoo portrait of Martin Luther King, Jr.

When Dutch tattooer Hanky Panky (Henk Schiffmacher) stated that gay guys always want something macho, he was right, in a broad sense. But what does that actually mean?

Part of the answer comes from looking first at what gay people don't get tattooed.

Generally speaking, gay people aren't going to get something that could be considered hateful. Only a few times have I ever done a tattoo featuring skulls, and I have never done a tattoo of blood-related imagery or of things bleeding. In all my years of tattooing, I've only done one

Grim Reaper tattoo, an image that is otherwise quite common, especially among the straight biker set.

(It should be pointed out that there are possible sociological or cultural qualifiers to my observations. Most of my clients have been over 30 years of age; most are "regular guys," or part of the large urban-style gay leather scene; gay skinheads weren't part of my clientele, for no other reason than there simply weren't that many in the San Francisco Bay Area.)

Being gay in America, especially in the twentieth century and beyond, has meant being a target of hatred, assault, and even murder. Gay history in this country is a history of police raids on gay bars, entrapment, families forcing their children to have lobotomies to "cure" them, and churches teaching shame and self-hatred. It's a history of incarceration, forced dishonesty, electroconvulsive treatments, chemical castration, dishonorable military discharges, employment and housing discrimination, threats of quarantine, being bullied in schools, brutal street murders, and gay teens committing suicide. Gay people watched in horror and frustration as friends and loved ones died all around them from a disease that politicians, evangelists, and the smug self-righteous said we deserved.

In the wake of the 1969 Stonewall Inn Riot in New York City, when a group of drag queens fought back during a police raid, gays stopped accepting the status quo and began adopting positive symbols representing pride and unity, made even stronger by the advent of AIDS. The rainbow flag and the AIDS quilt have become testaments to the strength and determination of a group that has for so long been considered less than equal by the rest of society.

Of course, not every gay person gets a tattoo that directly shouts "Hey — I'm gay." Gay people do, however, almost invariably choose positive imagery that strengthens and celebrates a sense of self-worth as a human being, on both a personal and a social level. The iconography may vary, but the intent is the same whether or not the tattoos can be labeled "queer."

The rainbow colors associated with gay pride since the late 1970s are probably the most recognized gay statement in the world and have been incorporated into all manner of queer tattoo imagery from rainbow flag tattoos to rainbow angel wings to rainbow bears and bear paw-prints to tennis balls to barcodes to cigars with rainbow smoke. The Greek lower-case lambda, symbol of the Gay Activist Alliance since its founding in December, 1969, was also incorporated into gay tattoos.

As AIDS progressed, other images also became important symbols of gay pride and AIDS activism, and these too became part of the gay tattoo lexicon.

During World War II homosexuals in Nazi concentration camps were forced to wear inverted pink triangle badges, similar to how a yellow Star of David identified Jews. When the Nazi concentration camps were liberated by the Allies, homosexuals were forced to serve the rest of their sentence.

In 1987 the Silence=Death Project mounted posters in New York which featured an upright pink triangle against a black background and the words "Silence=Death" in large white letters. The slogan was aimed at those who were unwilling to discuss or promote safe-sex practices or who were unwilling to speak up about social and governmental injustices. Later, the logo was adopted by the protest group ACT UP. Particularly through the 1990s tattoos incorporating pink triangles were nearly as frequent as rainbow flag tattoos.

With the onslaught of AIDS the question of whether or not, or when, to disclose one's HIV status to potential sex partners became a matter of considerable debate, generating a nearly endless stream of articles and op-ed pieces. Tangentially, condom use (safe sex) versus unprotected sex (barebacking) has also been an ongoing topic for debate, and that debate is now just as lively among heterosexuals. Safe sex practices and education became more prominent during the late 1980s as a result of the AIDS epidemic. The 1984 decision to shut down San Francisco's bath houses and sex clubs ignored what was, in reality, an enormous educational potential.

Amongst gays the universal biohazard symbol took on a new dimension as an indicator of HIV-positive status. Some wore it as an activist statement while others who felt a moral and ethical obligation to be up-front about their HIV status also adopted it as a tattoo. Such openness could have its drawbacks, however, even in the gay community. One of my East Coast clients had me put the symbol on his arm only to have me cover it up on his next visit because of the strong negative reactions he received when he would go out to the bars.

If a man had to be hospitalized or put in a hospice due

to AIDS, it wasn't uncommon for family members to swoop in and try to dictate medical decisions whether or not there was a partner, or in spite of advance medical directives such as living wills or durable powers of attorney. On more than one occasion I was asked to prominently tattoo the phrase "Do Not Resuscitate, Do Not Intubate," usually on the person's chest.

In 1991, the red ribbon symbol indicating sympathy and support for those with HIV/AIDS was introduced at that year's Tony Awards ceremony. Designed by the graphic arts activist group Visual AIDS, red ribbons were being worn by prominent entertainers and by some national political figures including former California Governor Jerry Brown and First Lady Barbara Bush. The ribbon idea caught on and other groups designated variously-colored ribbons for their own causes, such as pink for breast cancer awareness and lime for non-Hodgkin's lymphoma awareness. There are now more than 40 ribbon types, and across the country they have become tattoo material for all kinds of people with loved ones who have been affected.

Historically, openly gay men have usually been perceived as effeminate. Since Shakespeare's time, flamboyantly effeminate men have been referred to as "queens." King James I's sexual orientation was so widely known that Sir Walter Raleigh is credited with remarking that "King Elizabeth" had been succeeded by "Queen James" (Catherine D. Bowen, *The Lion and the Throne*). Philippe I, Duke of Orléans and brother of French monarch Louis XIV, was an openly effeminate gay man despite his duty-bound marriage and children. By the mid-1700s in Britain

the exclusively gay Macaroni Club became the reference for
the derogatory British tune "Yankee Doodle."

Effeminacy in men flies in the face of socially accepted
male gender roles as family provider, hunter, leader, warrior,
and protector. While male effeminacy itself doesn't mean
that an effeminate man is gay, the general perception is that
he is at least something of a sissy. Furthermore, effeminate
gay men were perceived to be sad, lonely, desperate failures
engaged in stereotypical non-masculine occupations such as
hairdresser or interior designer or florist. Known generally
as "sweater queens" or "flamers," they were fans of Judy
Garland and opera diva Maria Callas; they spoke "girly"
talk and walked with a mincing gait; they had little poodles,
used smelly colognes, and wore flashy rings on manicured
fingers.

There have, of course, always been masculine gay men,
but they remained under the radar, and many preferred it
that way. Some were, of course, closeted and perhaps even
married, but there were others who simply found what they
needed in less obvious ways. I learned one of these ways in
a remarkable conversation with my grandmother.

During a visit to San Francisco with my first lover I
had purchased a small pendant, cast in silver, of two men
engaged in doggie-style anal sex, and I happened to be
wearing it later on when we went to visit my grandmother.
When she spotted it, she remarked, "Oh — looks like
prospectors." Puzzled by her matter-of-fact comment, I
asked what she meant.

Prescott, Arizona, was at one time a rather wild little

town complete with gambling and prostitutes and similar sinful things which were readily available along a one-block section of South Montezuma Street, famously referred to as "Whiskey Row" which, during its heyday, sported more than 40 saloons. During the 1920s and 1930s my grandmother had worked in a cafe on Whiskey Row and had become friends with a few of the prostitutes, many of whom were known to grub-stake prospectors or invest in other business ventures.

She explained that it wasn't uncommon for prospectors to come into town in pairs — in other words, they were couples who worked their claims, came in for supplies, maybe even shared a prostitute to liven things up a bit. That they were a queer couple was an unspoken understanding. It's not difficult, therefore, to infer that many so-called mountain men, itinerant drovers, and other loners had found that they could more easily be themselves away from the usual social climate.

Gay bikers and gay motorcycle clubs such as The Satyrs had been around since the 1950s, an offshoot of the larger post-war biker movement in this country. Credited as the beginnings of the gay S&M and leather subculture, these clubs and their members represented a small, relatively hidden portion of the gay population, existing primarily in larger urban settings such as Los Angeles, San Francisco, Chicago, and New York City.

But by the mid-1970s young gay men across the country were forming and defining a specifically masculine sub-culture which stressed gender conformity to "traditional" hegemonic masculinity. Culturally, we already had hyper-masculine examples in movie legends Marlon Brando, James Dean, and Steve McQueen, as well as the Marlboro Man cigarette advertising phenomenon. Since the early 1950s images of beautiful, youthful masculinity had been available from legendary physique photographers Bob Mizer, Bruce Bellas, Mel Roberts, and Jim French (aka Rip Colt). The concept of the "gay clone" came onto the scene from a variety of intersecting influences, several of which had been present for decades.

The stereotypical "Castro Clone" strove to emulate "manliness" and everything that went with it. He was the very picture of widely accepted definitions of masculinity. He was smooth, slim, and muscular from all those hours at the gym. He usually sported a mustache and wore working-class clothing that emphasized his physical attributes. His well-worn tight-fitting Levi 501 5-button jeans might even have been sanded at the knees and crotch in order to accentuate that worn look. He wasn't a biker, but he might wear fashion leathers when venturing South of Market. He was the ideal of gay porn films and gay monthly magazines such as *Mandate, Honcho,* and *Playguy.* He preferred to drink beer instead of pretty cocktails. He consciously adopted a masculine tone of voice. He went to the discos and danced the night away to "Macho Man," "YMCA," and "In The Navy" by the Village People. He was sexually wildly promiscuous, wearing T-shirts proclaiming "So Many Men — So Little Time."

A different Castro look, although not nearly as ubiquitous as the clone, was the All-American Boy. The embodiment of the idealized California surfer, he was a walking sex toy, usually seen wearing short shorts, long socks, and tennis shoes. He, too, was slender, muscular, and suitably tanned.

Tattoos and notions of masculinity have gone hand in hand for nearly two centuries now. The image of a sailor covered with tattoos had long been a staple of American myth and iconography. By contrast, the older, more genteel generation of gay men seldom had tattoos of any sort, and many wouldn't even dream of getting one. But for the new masculine sensibility tattoos played an enormous role in defining one's self.

Besides typical biker flames there are two tattoo motifs that have been around since the inception of biker clubs and which became common among gay bikers, later to be picked up by the clone set: barbed wire and chain, most often in the form of armbands. It's interesting to note here that neither of these iconic designs points to anything specifically gay. Instead, they could be viewed as among the first masculine-positive symbols adopted into gay male tattoo culture.

My very first barbed wire armband was carefully drawn, and I didn't make any errors in execution. I kept the drawing around for a long while, but over time I became dissatisfied with it. The barbs were evenly spaced, the wire elements between the barbs were thin, and the band was less than two inches high. In retrospect, it lacked the kind of bold "oomph" that could have made it a lot more convincing, more commanding. As I gained confidence I began free-handing barbed wire directly onto the skin with a ballpoint pen; I worked larger and bolder; I varied the direction that the barbs pointed, as well as the way the wires connected the barb units. One of the most satisfying pieces I did in this vein was a complete barbed wire harness.

At its most basic, a simple chain design requires two links: a "front" view (o) and a "side" view (-). When strung together the result is something like this: o-o-o-o-o-o-o-o-.

When making an armband, the side-view link is the connector for finishing the band as it straddles the adjacent front-view link. Simple. Just measure the distance around the arm, determine the number of 2-link units required, make the transfer, and slap it on. The problem is, it's not that simple, and that's true for any repeating pattern intended to be a band — Celtic knots, for instance, are an especial nightmare.

> *The Tattoo God's Universal Tattoo Truth #4:*
>
> *No matter how carefully you measure for an armband, when you go to put on the transfer there will be either an overlap or a gap.*

However you position the client when you measure — arm out, arm down, arm slightly away from the body, it simply doesn't matter — the client's arm will have mysteriously changed circumference by the time you get back to it. If the transfer overlaps by a bit, one can sometimes rectify that by asking the client to flex his arm slightly, thereby increasing the circumference, but if that's not enough, then it's necessary to make a new, shorter transfer. A gap can sometimes be reduced by wrapping the transfer tighter around the arm. I began calling this space the "fudge zone" and routinely placed it on the underside of the arm so that if I had to fudge the design slightly it wouldn't really be noticeable.

I didn't have an expensive copier, nor did I have a thermal transfer machine. Sometimes I had to trek back to Kinkos or the nearest office supply store, make new copies at a different size, and start over. One day I came up with a brilliant idea. I drew up a long chain and successively enlarged it at 2% increments. Now, armed with some 30 sizes of chain long enough to go around a football player's thigh, it was a lot easier to measure, compare, and trace for a new transfer.

There is an old saying that a black dress is always in fashion. Besides dragons, the most popular single tattoo design style among gay men has been "tribal" design — solid black abstract shapes and patterns derived from primitive, pre-technological tattoo styles.

Tattoo artist Leo Zulueta, who began tattooing professionally in 1981, is credited with being the father of modern tribal tattooing. His bold interpretations of designs from Borneo and Pacific Island groups widened then-current conceptions of tattooing and the appeal was instant — "tribal fever" reached every nook and cranny of the tattoo world. Some tattoo artists began to specialize in tribal interpretations, developing their own recognizable style. While most tribal work is non-representational, there are tribal interpretations of animal forms such as dragons, scorpions, and phoenixes.

Tribal-style tattoos perfectly suited gay men's masculine appreciation and concern with body image. Here was bold design for the sake of design, most often executed in solid black. The curves and angles of well-executed tribal design, whether large or small, serve to accent the contours of the body with a graceful flow, highlighting muscle structure and drawing attention to selected body parts. Here too was design that didn't shout "gay" — in fact, it didn't proclaim anything about the person beyond the fact that he bore a tattoo.

Another unique aspect of tribal design was that its appeal spanned numerous gay subgroups, from bikers to clones to spiritual/Wiccan groups like the Radical Faeries.

By the time I moved into my shop on Juniper Street, I was working on a tribal concept almost every other week. Over time I would sometimes weary of it and complain that if I had to do one more f*ck*ng tribal armband I would scream and hurt someone. But I did them anyway.

I've had clients who, when describing what they have in mind, even when it's tribal, tell me that the design I come up with for them has to be "masculine," or that they want "masculine" colors. Sometimes a client will bring in a magazine photo or digital image of a tattoo on a handsome, muscular guy illustrating what they have in mind. That's when I explain another universal tattoo truth:

The Tattoo God's Universal Tattoo Truth #5:

No tattoo will make you more masculine than you already are, no amount of tattooing will make you look like that person in the magazine photo, and pink is only a color. Get over it.

THE BEAR THING

Body image and standards of beauty aren't confined solely to straight culture, where women have been the most frequent targets — and victims — of prevailing physical ideals. More and more, Hollywood, advertising, and popular media have imposed stricter, equally unattainable standards of beauty on men, no matter their sexual orientation.

Just take a look at how an iconic boy's childhood toy has morphed since its introduction in 1964. G.I. Joe, the world's first action figure, was a normal guy at first, with a respectable, natural physique. But with each incarnation G.I. Joe became more distorted — not only more buffed, but finally with physical proportions that defy reality — a fantasy plastic testament to the result of huge quantities of anabolic steroids.

The down side of societal physical norms is that only a small percentage of people even remotely fit them. The gay ideal clone with his perfect six-pack abs, bubble butt, bulging muscles, and sized-to-kill endowment was (and still is) a pipe-dream yardstick used to judge not only others but ourselves.

By the late 1970s a different kind of gay guy slowly began to be generally recognized. He reminded one of a burly lumberjack. He ranged in size from somewhat stocky to downright big, although there were thinner versions. He was hairy, often with a beard. He might not have visible abs, and in some cases might not even be able to see his toes. He was not a slave to gay fashion but was masculine in his own right. And he wasn't necessarily young. In other words, he was a Bear.

Precisely when gay men began differentiating themselves as bears is obscure. For a July, 1979, *Advocate* article, author George Mazzei wrote the humorous "Who's Who in the Zoo: A Glossary of Gay Animals," in which he described bears as one of seven gay animal archetypes (the others are Pussycats, Pekes and Afghans, Owls, Gazelles, Cygnet Swans, and Marmosets).

Gradually, a collective gay bear identity was forming, and it happened in several places at once — Australia, Kansas, California, Chicago, and the DC/Baltimore area, to name a few. But two things transpired which gave the bear movement the impetus it needed to become a major gay subgroup: wide recognition and a place where like-minded people could congregate.

In San Francisco wide recognition came in the form of *Bear Magazine*. Richard Bulger and his partner Chris Nelson published the first issue of *Bear Magazine* in 1987. As the magazine grew they formed Brush Creek Media, and in 1994 moved their Mission district office and Bear Store to 367 9th Street in the South of Market District, practically in the middle of the gay leather zone, and around the corner from the Lone Star Saloon on Harrison Street.

As it happened, the Lone Star Saloon was ideal for the bear bunch. The Lone Star originally opened its doors on July 4, 1989, over on Howard Street at the corner of 7th. The location had once been a tiny cocktail lounge with a large red neon martini glass on the outside near the door. It quickly became home for the Rainbow Motorcycle Club. My friend "Bonsai Pete" Vafiades was bartending there and graciously provided this description:

> The doors were not self-closing and there was not a curtain, and due to the space being a bit below street level the sun would be directly in your eyes whenever anyone would walk in. Furthermore, anyone walking into the bar would be facing a dark interior and several steps downward, and inevitably they would fail to realize that the doors remained open after they walked in. The entire crowd would all scream, "Close The Fucking Door!" The original Lone Star Saloon T-shirt had this slogan across the back of it.

> After the [Loma Pieta] earthquake [three months later], the search began for a new location for the bar since the Howard Street building was damaged beyond repair and was immediately slated for demolition. There were very few possibilities at the time, but the one that did finally pan out was the old Juanita's on Harrison [across from the old Ambush]. The building had been sold to a man with the last name of Jarrin. He owned a T-shirt embroidering shop down on Brannan Street. He purchased the Harrison St. property and went about setting it up to become a sweat shop for manufacturing T-shirts and Ball Caps.

> When we first went to look at the place it was full of industrial sewing machines, and he had spent quite a lot of money upgrading

the electric service to accommodate the
planned production of garments. Evidently,
at some point, he ran into a problem with
the city issuing him permits to conduct his
business there, and so he decided to rent
the building out. Since the location had
previously been a bar, there was no problem
with the city allowing us to reopen the place
as a bar.

When owner Rick Redewill acquired the old Juanita's
I was fortunate enough to help get the place ready, and
the grand opening was certainly an event. The bar itself
wasn't even finished yet — I think it was still plywood.
The Rainbow Motorcycle Club had rolled their motorcycles
into the bar, and the new patrons could take their drinks to
a large back patio. It was festive indeed. Not only did the
RMC have a new home, but here was a place where lost-
soul Ambush regulars could again come together, almost
like old times.

Rick, like so many of us, happened to be a big fan of
the animated TV sitcom "The Simpsons," which had first
aired on the Fox network just a few months earlier. Shown
regularly on a big television screen in the bar, patrons loved
the satirical social commentary and the non-judgmental
inclusion of gay characters — something quite novel for
television programming at the time.

From the outset, what distinguished the Lone Star
Saloon was that, like the Ambush, it wasn't a typical South
of Market leather bar. One of the great hallmarks of both
bars was inclusivity — anyone was welcome as long as he
left his attitude outside. It wasn't long before the bear bunch

realized they had a place to call theirs, and they gravitated to it like, well, bears to a salmon run. The central location of both the Bear Store and the Lone Star Saloon facilitated this — motels and hotels were within easy walking distance, and the annual Folsom Street Fair was practically on their doorsteps.

Across the country the bear movement took off big-time, with events, codes, bear clubs, and a culture-specific identity, all within less than a decade. There is even a Bear Pride flag, designed by Craig Byrnes in 1995. Naturally, it wasn't long before different sorts of bears came to be recognized:

Otter: a man who is hairy but not heavy.

Cub: a relatively young bear. The term also refers to a bear's husband/partner who takes the passive role in the relationship.

Daddy Bear: a mature, older bear, who is often looking for a Cub for a relationship.

Grizzly Bear: an extremely tall, heavy or hairy bear; may be quite dominant.

Polar Bear: a bear with white or grey hair.

Panda Bear: an Asian bear.

Black Bear: an African-American bear.

Brown Bear: a Latino bear.

Koala Bear: an Australian bear.

Pocket Bear: a bear with a small build.

Chubby Bear: a bear who is quite heavy-set and hairy.

Wolf: a bear who is rugged and outdoorsy, but is likely also a biker.

> Goldilocks: a woman who hangs out with bears.
> This is the Bear culture's equivalent of a "fag
> hag."

The bear phenomenon also rapidly found its way into gay tattoo iconography. Stylized bear paw prints have remained steadily popular as stand-alone designs, incorporated into armbands, or as one element of larger designs. One kind of tattoo I always thought would be fun, but haven't done, is a bear paw-print version of dance step diagrams like tango or waltz or foxtrot.

Both northwest and southwest Native American bear-related art has been frequently borrowed for tattoos. Teddy bears of all sorts remain popular, and the dancing bears from the rock group Grateful Dead are an easy armband choice. Bear tattoos I've done over the years include growling bears and peaceful bears; tribal-design bears, cartoon bears, and rainbow bears; polar bears, brown bears, black bears, grizzlies, and koala bears; military service bears, and bears wearing camouflage; elaborate Celtic braid bears; hear, see, and speak-no-evil bears; biker bears, cowboy bears, and Winnie the Pooh.

CANCER

For some time I had been experiencing daily bouts of heartburn, which grew steadily worse. Bicarbonate of soda and Alka-Seltzer were constant companions. Without medical insurance or a regular doctor I took the typical guy approach of ignoring whatever was going on. But in early August, 1992, I felt so bad that I stayed in bed for a couple of days, not eating, and drinking only some Gatorade. Then, in the evening, I felt something acutely strange happen in my belly. It wasn't particularly painful as pain goes, but I knew something was seriously not right.

The next day Tim's doctor agreed to see me. He poked and prodded, then sent me to Davies Medical Center for X-rays and blood work. Afterward, I waited around for a couple of hours, but with no immediate news I decided to take a cab home. By the time I got to the cottage there was a phone message to call the doctor. He wanted me to come back to the hospital and check in. When I said that I would wait until the next morning because it was already late in the day, he said, "Do it now!" Because I had no insurance and wasn't aware that I would have been admitted to Davies anyway, I decided to head over to San Francisco General. Within a matter of hours I was admitted and taken to surgery, still not knowing what the problem was.

Not only did I have colon cancer, but my intestine had ruptured. I came out of anesthesia with Tim at my side, to discover that my abdomen was heavily bandaged from sternum to pubic bone and that I had an ostomy "appliance" glued to a hole in my side — in other words, a colostomy bag. I was put in a room with one other patient, who kept the window curtains drawn. To make matters even more gloomy, I learned the next day that my good friend Snowflake had succumbed to AIDS. I could only lie there and bawl.

The prognosis wasn't very good, and I was put on an immediate one-year weekly chemotherapy regimen. During a three-month period I underwent a total of four separate surgeries, the last one fortunately being a "take down" to reconnect everything so that I wouldn't have to live with the bag. I had dropped nearly 40 pounds. So that I wouldn't have to stay in the hospital, I learned to change my own dressings twice daily using a wet-to-dry technique in which moist gauze is applied to the wound and, when dry, pulls dead tissue and wound drainage with it when it is removed. It's a slow healing process.

I believe that my irrepressible sense of humor kept me from total depression. While I was wearing that stupid bag, I recall suggesting to my sister that we could easily team up as jewel thieves — we could go to high-end shops on Rodeo Drive in Los Angeles, ask to see expensive unset gems, and while she diverted the salesperson's attention I could stash a handful in the bag — after all, who would want to dig through that?

Bills were stacking up, and to make matters more difficult, rumors were flying around that I had died. As soon as I could following the final surgery, I started working again, even though I could usually work for only an hour or so, especially on days following chemotherapy treatments.

Most tattoo clients, especially regulars, were understanding and cooperative. But there's always someone who just has to push the limits.

"Trevor," an Englishman who was taking classes at the San Francisco Art Institute, came in to get a piece colored in — a large dragon that had been outlined by London tattooer George Bone. It wound around his entire right leg, with the tail on his instep and the head extending around most of his upper leg, its horns just below his genitals. The only way to work on the upper inside of his leg was for him to lie on my bench with his right leg up over my shoulder, requiring me to hunch forward under the weight of his leg, a rather grueling process. While I was working in this way, he would get an erection, which I ignored. At one point I became quite light-headed and quickly realized that he was sniffing poppers while I worked! I had to stop and told him firmly that I simply wasn't able to work that way and that he would need to keep his kinks at home or not return.

The Tattoo God's Universal Tattoo Truth #6:

When you least expect it, somebody's getting off.

A month or so later Trevor managed to piss me off yet again when he brought in a friend who was visiting from London. I don't remember what he wanted. When they both arrived for the appointment, it was obvious that they had been partying heavily. I had barely started work on the friend, when he became pale and asked for some water. He gulped down a big glass of water and then proceeded to vomit all over the room. Their apologies fell on deaf ears. Enough was enough. I refused to see Trevor or his friend again.

When clients made an appointment I would remind them not to consume alcohol or aspirin for a day or two in advance, because these act as blood thinners. "Marvin" was getting a modest tribal piece on his left arm, and I was puzzled because he was bleeding quite a lot while I worked. I switched out the needle group, thinking that perhaps I had overlooked a bent needle tip, but he still bled far more than would be normal. When I asked if he had been drinking or taking aspirin, he told me that he took three 325 mg aspirins every morning because he had read that a daily aspirin regimen reduces risk of heart attacks. I told him that not only was that a dumb-ass idea, but he would need to wait a few days to finish the project, because that much bleeding was certain to spoil his healing.

The vast majority of my clients were great guys, and I tend to be a trusting soul, so I seldom asked for a deposit on design work. Now and then, however, my little inner voice would say, "be careful."

An older gentleman, accompanied by a much younger companion, came to talk about a Samoan-style tattoo that would wrap around his upper legs and waist, somewhat like golf shorts. He had been on a diet for some time, had lost a great deal of weight, and said he wanted to celebrate his weight loss. The problem, however, was that the loose skin on his abdomen and legs hung in numerous floppy folds, so I told him that his idea was ill-advised. He was insistent that something could be done, but I was suspicious, so I said that I would require a cash deposit to begin drawings. Assuring me that he would go to the bank and be back shortly, they left and I never saw them again.

The Tattoo God's Universal Tattoo Truth #7:

There is always someone with a tattoo idea you never imagined.

Over the course of a couple of years I had corresponded periodically with a fellow who told me he wanted to be tattooed head to toe, so that he would look like the Creature From the Black Lagoon, a monster from the 1954 film of the same name. He had sent photos and described his rather elaborate ideas of how to make his face and hands resemble the monster's as much as possible. He even telephoned a couple of times. After a while, though, I began to suspect that he wasn't that serious, so I stopped replying to him (see Universal Tattoo Truth #6).

Then one day I got a surprise call from him. He was in town and wanted to begin the project. Because chemo days were so exhausting, I had to schedule his appointment for the day after my chemotherapy session, but he and the friend he was with said that was no problem. They were staying at a motel a fair distance from my studio, and I briefly stopped by after my session to meet them. We set a time for early the next day, and I even offered to drive over to the motel to pick them up for the appointment. When I got there, however, they had already checked out and departed. I never heard from the guy again.

HOMOEROTICA

Gay or straight, guys love their porn, and guys love erotic tattoos. It's a guy thing. Women do get erotic tattoo art pieces, of course, but not nearly at the rate that men get them. Erotic tattoos can range from small, amusing, cartoon-style pieces to large, high-quality artworks on skin.

Usually, a client would come to the studio with a magazine or book illustration by a well-known artist and ask for that to be copied, while at other times I was asked to draw something up for his particular concept.

The works of Touko Laaksonen (1920-1991), known to the world by his pseudonym "Tom of Finland," topped the list of most frequently requested erotic tattoos from known artists. His iconic, stylized images of ruggedly handsome leather men, swaggering bikers, over-endowed sailors, sweaty laborers, and sadistic law-enforcement officers captured the imagination of late 20th-century queer culture. Add to that his smooth, highly refined drawing style, and the result can be a masterpiece of subtle black-and-gray tattooing.

Another artist whose work translates quite nicely for tattooing was Chicago artist Etienne (Domingo Orejudos, 1933-1991). Like Tom of Finland's work, Etienne's books of drawings and his many posters for the famed Gold Coast bar in Chicago are testaments to rugged masculinity and gym-toned bodies. Details I especially like about his work are facial expressions and the way he drew hands and feet. His drawings aren't as highly polished as Tom's, but his line-drawing style and simplified shading translate perfectly into traditional tattoo interpretations. For one such tattoo, I reworked a piece of 1950s flash by Sailor Jerry Collins, replacing the pinup girl with one of Etienne's hunks while keeping the rest of it just as Collins drew it.

Across three continents the pointillist work of porn noir artist REX has been used to promote leather parties, poppers, leather and fetish gear, hotel accommodations, sex clubs, and even condoms. His vision of queer sex and sleaze springs from settings of hidden t-rooms, shoddy hotels with peeling wallpaper and graffiti, back alleys, and all the other dark places which echo the shadow-world of gay sexual fantasy — a world of beer cans, cigarettes, jock straps, glory holes, bare light bulbs, old mattresses, rusty plumbing, "greaser" hair styles, and, of course, tattoos.

Had he wished, REX could have been a great tattooer. The designs on his figures aren't just hasty representations of any old piece of ink. They are immaculate little gems, some interpretive, others quite original, and they glow with the best qualities of tattoo conception: tight design perfectly balancing elements of dark and light, as well as provocative body placement.

REX's style of pointillism, sometimes called "stipple," is in the tradition of the great pen-and-ink illustrators such as Virgil Finlay, Wallace Wood, and Berni Wrightson. The use of dots to build form is readily adaptable to tattooing and works well in combination with standard techniques.

Other artists whose work people brought in have included queer artists Domino, Zach, the Hun, Harry Bush,

A-Jay, Roger Payne, Minoru, *Drummer* magazine artist Bill Ward, and French poet, artist, and filmmaker Jean Cocteau. Leonardo da Vinci's *Vitruvian Man* has been used in countless ways, and the central figure has sometimes been altered to represent chunky bear-types, leather clones, and in one instance, I did a version as a teddy bear wearing a harness. While not himself gay, English Art Nouveau illustrator and author Aubrey Beardsley's grotesque erotica has often appealed to gay sensibilities.

At age 75, "Daniel" was the oldest client I had ever worked with. When he arrived at the studio he was the very picture of respectability, with a quiet, pleasant demeanor. The purpose of his visit was that he wanted to get some old marks on his legs covered up.

When he disrobed, my assessment of Daniel took a whole new turn. On the center of his chest was a large scimitar, which had been done by Cliff Raven. On either side of his abdomen was a stylized image of a leatherman, designed by legendary gay porn artist REX, also executed by Cliff Raven. He turned around. On his right shoulder blade was a naked man in bondage. On each cheek of his buttocks was a large, ugly black star. But the mind-boggling part was a hodgepodge of irregular ugly dark scratch marks one-half to two inches long scattered all over his groin, extending onto the insides of his legs, and wrapping around onto his buttocks, encompassing an area that could be more or less covered by a pair of golf shorts.

As his story unfolded, I learned that he was a Catholic priest living in the Midwest, who necessarily kept his tattoos hidden. He was also a complete masochist. The ugly stars on his buttocks had been his first tattoos, done late one night in New Orleans by a drunk, straight tattooer, because Daniel thought the guy was sexy. The ugly random marks had been done over a period of months by a boyfriend who would dip an icepick in ink and then make random scratch marks. Daniel wanted me to come up with a cover for these marks, but only with black and gray — no color.

I told him that it wouldn't be possible to completely cover all those marks and suggested that it would be better to detract from that mess by doing something large and very bold, like jumbo barbed wire. He liked that idea, and we got started. He also wanted to begin adding to the work on his back. He had brought with him a few magazines with S&M drawings and illustrations to show what he had in mind.

I worked on Daniel about every 6 months for over 4 years, and we became friends. He would come to the City for a week's stay, take in theatre and art museums, then end his visit with a day-long tattoo session. Each time he would bring along some more magazines with illustrations to use for his back piece, which eventually became an interesting collage of S&M art. He always left those magazines with me, because he was reluctant to keep them in his room where he lived lest they be discovered. He always sent a Christmas card. Finally, he sent a letter saying that his health was failing and that he wouldn't be continuing his tattoo work. Eventually, we didn't hear from him anymore. I often wondered how his priest colleagues reacted when they found out about his secret.

Yet another interesting project was for a 40-something man who was gay but who got turned on by straight porn.

Like my priest friend Daniel, he would bring in various photos and illustrations from porn magazines. Quite closeted, he cautioned me to be very discreet whenever I called him, because he lived with his mom, and together they raised parakeets (which I could always hear in the background). If his mother answered the phone, I was to say I was calling about his doctor appointment.

Some guys wanted cartoon-character erotica, and these playful, light-hearted pieces are always fun to do. While I haven't conducted any formal research on the topic, I would be willing to wager that the history of this kind of tattoo goes quite a ways back, based on historic photos I've seen, tattoo flash of Sailor Jerry Collins, and the popularity of "Tijuana Bibles" — small porn comics that circulated mostly during the Depression Era and featured plagiarized "Sunday Funnies" characters doing all manner of lewd things.

"Bugs" was hugely fond of Warner Brothers cartoon characters, and his homoerotica project was certainly one of those once-in-a-career experiences.

When I first met Bugs he had a tattoo of a grinning Bugs Bunny on his penis, a cartoon butterfly on the glans, and a couple of patchy-looking heart tattoos on his scrotum. Initially, he wanted to refurbish the heart tattoos and add a couple more.

He then decided that he wanted me to come up with homoerotic versions of his favorite characters to be placed on his crotch and buttocks, with the idea that all these would be contained within a space covered by his briefs.

Yosemite Sam is "porking" Porky Pig. Daffy Duck has balls that drag the ground. Bugs Bunny is using a carrot as a dildo. Other characters include Foghorn Leghorn, Marvin the Martian, Speedy Gonzales, Wiley Coyote, and the Roadrunner. Yosemite Sam, Daffy Duck, and the Tasmanian Devil are arranged over his pubic area with lettering that reads "Party Animal."

His other tattoos were much tamer, and you would never know of the cartoon orgy under his briefs unless he let you in on his secret world.

1993 – 1996

Finally! No more chemotherapy. For months, I had gone in weekly for an intravenous "push" of a thick, syrupy fluid called Fluorouracil, or 5-FU. One of the immediate side effects was immense fatigue. I would get home and sleep the rest of the day. Added to this for three days every other week was a pill called Levamisole, and that stuff would knock me on my ass.

I jokingly complained about Levamisole to my oncology doctor, telling him that I believed it would undoubtedly induce labor in rhinos and other large mammals. He told me that Levamisole was originally developed to treat worm infestations in cattle, pigs, and sheep. I allowed as how I was certainly grateful to know that I was at least free of worms.

On one of my treatment days my nurse told me of a boy who had recently gone through a surgery similar to mine. She explained that he was seriously depressed about having a colostomy bag, albeit temporary. I volunteered to visit him and talk to him a little while, so she arranged for the boy's mother to call me. I wasn't sure what I could say to the kid that others hadn't said, so I took along a gift for him: a teddy bear to which I had attached a little zippered bag filled with jelly beans. We had a great visit, and his mom was terrific.

While the year of chemotherapy was uncomfortable, I actually didn't have it so bad. Whenever I went to the hospital ward for my treatments, there were others there who were clearly in far worse circumstances. Some of them were in beds or wheelchairs with IV tubes in their arms that dripped medication over a span of hours. Nothing I was going through could have measured up against what these people were enduring, and I was filled with compassion for them.

Without the hassle of chemotherapy, work at last settled into a pleasant routine. Because of my agreement with the landlady not to have evening clients, I booked two or maybe three appointments a day beginning at nine in the morning. Usually I finished the day by around six in the evening but would work later if it was a large project or something for an out-of-town client where project time was limited. Even though I tried to reserve Mondays for a day off, that didn't always happen. Typically, tattoo shops open late and stay open late into the night, but the difference didn't seem to noticeably affect my business, maybe because gay guys generally like to reserve their evenings for socializing.

Any couple that has been together for any length of time develops its own traditions that are meaningful to them. Tim and I had no enthusiasm for the holidays, so we would usually have a couple of friends over for a non-traditional meal that might only be pizza. Our most meaningful annual event was our anniversary, which we calculated to be the last day of September. I'm not sure just when we started going to our favorite Chinese restaurant, Henry's Hunan on Sansome Street between Broadway and Vallejo, but that became our annual ritual. We always ordered the same thing: onion cake, dumplings, and a smoked ham dish called "Marty's Special."

The 1993 big-budget drama film *Philadelphia*, starring Tom Hanks and Denzel Washington, was a powerfully visceral examination of homophobic responses to homosexuality and HIV/AIDS. That a major Hollywood studio took on the topic at the time was itself something of a gamble, as this was the first high-profile film to seriously explore AIDS. The story, about an AIDS victim who sues his law firm for wrongful termination, helped bring the social issues surrounding AIDS to a huge audience. His performance in the role of main character Andrew Beckett earned Tom Hanks his second Academy Award Oscar.

Widespread misinformation and fears about transmission of AIDS and hepatitis meant that the burgeoning tattoo industry was finding itself under more scrutiny from health officials and lawmakers, many of whom had at best sketchy notions about the tattooing process, had never seen a tattoo applied, and who believed that most tattooers were among the ranks of ruthless con artists and ex-convicts. While most states imposed a minimum age for tattooing, they let their counties deal with regulating tattooing practices, and those regulations varied wildly from county to county, even within a single state. One county might ban tattooing within any city limits, so tattooers would set up in trailers just outside the city limits. I recall reading that one county in Florida stipulated that any tattooing required a licensed doctor to be present. Tattooers themselves, having no consistent set of industry standards to go by, were left to their own methods for meeting county requirements and assuring their customers and local officials of their safe practices.

The Alliance of Professional Tattooists (APT), founded in 1992, was formed to address that lack of industry-wide standards, educate tattooers and legislators alike, and provide accurate up-to-date information to its members. I signed up and began receiving their newsletter, *Skin Scribe*, which included articles on health and safety issues and business-related information.

I was honored to be one of more than eighty tattoo artists chosen nationwide whose work was included in the 1995 New York exhibition *Pierced Hearts and True Love: A Century of Drawings for Tattoos*, curated by famed tattooer Don Ed Hardy and staged by the Drawing Center. The show subsequently traveled to other cities in the U.S. and Canada, including San Francisco at the Yerba Buena Center. When I got the printed catalog, however, I was surprised to see that I and more than twenty other participating artists had not been included. I still have the three drawings that were in that show, stored in the same packages in which they were returned.

When I was drafted into military service during the Vietnam conflict, the Uniform Code of Military Justice banned homosexuals from serving in the Armed Forces and had strict discharge rules for those service members found to be homosexual. Of course, that didn't stop homosexual activity in the military, but it certainly made things doubly punitive for those who were caught or who admitted to being homosexual.

As part of his 1992 Presidential campaign, Bill Clinton promised to lift that ban. The opposition was predictably intense, with claims that homosexual service members would demoralize straight personnel, that straight personnel would never be comfortable showering with homosexuals, and that God certainly didn't like the idea one bit.

In a compromise which came to be known as "Don't Ask, Don't Tell," President Bill Clinton issued a defense directive in December, 1993, that military applicants could not be asked about their sexual orientation. Sometimes a compromise doesn't go far enough in helping those it is intended to help, but at least it made some headway. It would take another seventeen years for Don't Ask, Don't Tell to at last be overturned during President Barak Obama's first Presidential term.

At the time no state recognized same-sex marriage, and the notion that gays and lesbians might ever be able to marry legally in this country was considered by most to be just a pipe dream. But there were currents of support. In Hawaii lawmakers and activists were actively pursuing the marriage equality dream, and this became a matter of grave concern for conservatives and liberals alike, especially during the 1996 Presidential campaigns.

Republicans and far-right religious groups saw an easy political wedge issue and took full advantage of it. If straight marriage and the "traditional family" were an Oreo cookie, gay marriage was the 18-wheeler that would surely crush them out of existence. Engineered by Georgia Republican Senator Newt Gingrich, the Defense Of Marriage Act (DOMA) was passed by the Senate on September 10, 1996. Caving to political expediency, Bill Clinton signed it into law late in the night. There would be no federal recognition of same-sex marriage until 2013 and the historic Supreme Court rulings striking down key provisions of DOMA.

PART MAN, PART BEAST

A ncient Greek and Near-Eastern mythologies gave us some fantastic semi-human creatures which are part human and part some other animal. Of these, centaurs, angels, mermen, satyrs and fauns, and the Minotaur have been among the most frequently adapted to gay erotica and gay erotic tattooing.

Trying to draw these things, however, is particularly challenging, even when working from available reference material. The human imagination easily accepts that a centaur is a human head, arms, and torso attached to the body of a horse, or that an angel is a human body with a bird's wings.

But each of these is actually an artist's orthopedic nightmare. For a centaur, just how much of the human torso does one use? Where does it join with the horse? Is the navel included on the human part? Never mind that a centaur apparently has two hearts, two pairs of lungs, two sets of intestines, and a dangerously extended spine.

The centaur for "Carlton" is a case in point, revolving around Carlton's fetish for muscles, rumps, and exaggerated genitals. He had made a primitive sketch showing the centaur from behind, not a typical pose at all. The human part was turned back to show a full face, broad manly pectorals and the requisite six-pack abs. The centaur also carried a bow, while a quiver of arrows was slung over one shoulder.

My first task was to point out to Carlton that the

human part couldn't possibly twist far enough around for both pectorals to be equally visible. Another task was how to position the horse's tail so that it didn't obscure the exaggerated genitals. And, just to complicate things a bit more, the centaur's face was to be Carlton's likeness. Thankfully, I have an excellent book of comparative anatomy, and I was able to round up a couple of books with pictures of horses. Carlton reluctantly compromised on the anatomy issues, and I did manage to come up with a quite nice piece of work.

When you think about it, an angel is a human body with six limbs. How, and just where, does one convincingly attach wings on an angel? In order to carry the weight of the body in flight, an angel's wingspan should ideally be approximately double the angel's height, meaning that an angel six feet tall would have to have at least a twelve-foot wingspan. Additionally, the angel's chest muscles, like those of any flying bird, would have to be enormously developed if the angel actually intends to fly successfully.

Another thing that always puzzled me about angels is that they are, one would assume, mammals. Now, the only mammals that actually fly, as distinguished from gliding, are bats. So, technically, why wouldn't angels have bat-like wings instead of feathered wings?

"Harry" wanted an angel in flight on the left side of his chest. Since I felt that it should follow something of an arc on his pectoral, I was able to find a suitable image in a book of Gustav Doré illustrations for Dante's Divine Comedy, and added wings that flowed along the arc. The total image wasn't over eight inches altogether, and was in black and gray. Harry asked if I could make the features resemble those of his boyfriend Jorge, a handsome young man from Guatemala, with a face resembling ancient classic Mayan sculpture. Even though the angel's face was only about an inch high at best, it wasn't difficult to portray the characteristic broad nose and high cheekbones. But I had to laugh out loud when Harry asked if I could include Jorge's "dreamy eyelashes."

I guess it goes with the territory, but I have yet to tattoo a classic mermaid on virtually anybody. I have, however, done numerous mer-*men*, including the Greek god Poseidon with his beard and trident, riding a dolphin. Compared to other gay erotica, depictions of mermen have tended to be more light-hearted, even coy and playful. Drawing these is somewhat easier, too. It has always been interesting to me how the client wanted the tail depicted — sometimes the tail is simple, sometimes similar to a dolphin tail, and sometimes more elaborate and wavy like the tails on some varieties of fancy goldfish. There may or may not be additional small fins at the elbow, or a fin on the merman's head, in the manner of a mohawk. It's also interesting to note that the matter of whether or not to add human male genitalia has been about a 50-50 split.

For the most part the technical differences distinguishing satyrs from fauns isn't of great concern to the average tattoo client. Rather, it is the generalized part-man, part-goat concept that stirs the imagination. For the artist, these are far easier to conceive, because there aren't the outrageous skeletal inconsistencies inherent in the other kinds of half-man, half-beast creatures. After all, if people can walk around in stiletto heels, geta sandals, ballet slippers, platform shoes, or knee-high lace-up steel-toe boots, it's entirely plausible for a human to walk on cloven hooves.

Fauns and especially satyrs could be considered the original party animals, fitting right in with the sex, drugs, and rock-and-roll crowd. The Greek goat-god Pan (a faun) is of particular interest because of his incredible virility and uncivilized sex-for-the-sake-of-sex lust. But Pan, it turns out, is a far more complex creature. Jungian psychologist James Hillman, in his fascinating book *Pan and the Nightmare*, shows us that Pan is also the god of masturbation, rape, nightmares, and panic attacks. Every tattoo I did of a Pan/satyr/faun, of course, featured a large, uncircumcised phallus.

In Greek legend the Minotaur was a monster son of King Minos of Crete, with the head of a bull on a man's body. Kept in a labyrinth, the Minotaur routinely devoured Athenian boys and girls sent to King Minos as payment for the assassination of his oldest son and was eventually killed by Theseus, the founder-king of Athens. There are countless beautiful illustrations of the Minotaur, most of them stressing its strength and ferocity. In gay erotica, it is of course also immensely sexual, and by inference, would have presented a much different sort of threat to Theseus.

I've done only a couple of werewolf tattoos. On one other occasion, the client wanted a creature with the body of a man and head of a cougar.

A DAY AT THE ZOO

Early man's first artwork concerns itself with two main things: himself and other animals. Animals, after all, are creatures more or less like us — our nearest neighbors in creation's panoply of living things. We raise them or hunt them; we eat them; we put them to work or keep them around as pets; we employ their products — flesh, bones, skin, teeth, and even their manure. More than that, we have imbued them with personalities and character traits and have given them key roles in our creation myths. We have identified, often as groups, with perceived attributes of a chosen animal: strength, temperament, beauty, ferocity, ability. In fact, we still do. In sports we have the Cal Bears, Miami Dolphins, Atlanta Falcons, and Philadelphia Eagles. A donkey and an elephant symbolize our major political parties, while a bull and a bear testify to our economic ups and downs.

Since ancient times animal images have been called upon to fill an apotropaic function in that we summon, through the image itself, aspects of a creature's ferocity, wisdom, and skill to protect us from real or imaginary dangers.

Thanks to tattooing we have one of the earliest and most amazingly sophisticated examples of just such a function. In the 1940s the frozen 2000-year-old remains of a Scythian warrior were discovered in the Altai region of Southern Siberia. Based on the size of his gravesite, the artifacts that were buried with him, the obvious attempts to mummify and preserve his flesh, along with the extensive tattoo work covering his body, he was doubtless an important man in his day.

A great fish swims up his leg. A ram dances around his arm, along with curiously-beaked deer and other fanciful creatures. An odd arrangement of dots parallel either side of his lower spine. Whoever did the tattooing was certainly aware of calculated placement to correspond with musculature and physical motion.

One of the most fascinating of these is the likeness of a cat, whose barred tail is cunningly wrapped around the left shoulder blade, while its body goes along the upper ribs under the arm, with the head situated on the left pectoral muscle (the head is assumed here, since the warrior's remains were damaged in some spots). This is a very odd placement, but consider what it might accomplish during battle: at the precise moment that our warrior raises his weapon, his enemy is momentarily transfixed by what he sees jumping out at him. That brief psychological advantage is all it takes to make the difference between victory or death. I confess that this is strictly my own theory, and I couldn't possibly prove the correlation between the placement of the tattoo and any advantage in battle. Additionally, my little theory also leaves open to speculation whether or not this warrior was left-handed (as he might be holding his shield with his right hand).

Most modern tattooed people are probably not going to be running around fighting naked with swords and spears and such, but the ancient notion of carrying certain protective images on one's body is still around.

With the exception of pigs, there are no specifically gay

connotations to these animals (that I know of). However, they have been requested with sufficient frequency for me to include them.

• A Convocation of Eagles. For more than a century the eagle has dominated Western tattoo animal iconography. As an archetypal image it is a symbol of height, is identified with the sun and male energy, and is frequently a father symbol. Noted for its speed and its daring in flight, it has since Roman times been associated with gods of power and war. (J. E. Cirlot, *Dictionary of Symbols*, pp 91, 92).

In the gay community the eagle is one of the most popular images. It seems as though wherever there is a sizable gay community there is also a bar called the Eagle — San Francisco; New York City; Boston; Seattle; Washington, D.C.; Las Vegas; and Amsterdam.

Eagles are a worldwide staple of the tattooer's repertoire, sometimes to the point of being boring. Pointing out that there are other interesting birds of prey which can be artistically rendered usually elicits a blank stare. And, invariably, the eagle must be HEROIC. It seems to jar people's sensibilities when I suggest that maybe the eagle could be dramatically tearing up the Energizer Bunny or perhaps electrocuting itself on a power line.

• A Pantheon of Panthers. The language of gay tattooing very early on adopted the famous black panther, among the most ubiquitous tattoo designs of the mid-20th century. Introduced by Milwaukee tattooer Amund Dietzel in 1939, I believe it is one of the most ingenious designs ever conceived for the human body. When sized correctly and well placed its sinuous S-shape is perfectly adapted to complement a muscle mass. No matter how the person wearing it moves, the panther moves almost magically with him in a fluid rhythm, like an intuitive dance partner.

• A Pride of Lions. My favorite lion tattoo was of the head of a lion smoking a cigar, the smoke trail wafting up through its mane. My initial drawing had been done with a blue pencil. A few years later, just for fun, I scanned the drawing and made it the central piece of a computer-designed cigar box design: "Blue Lion Cigars."

• An Ambush of Tigers. Tigers are great tattoo images because of their stripes, and tiger heads are notable because, in color, tiger noses are frequently pink, whereas lions have dark noses. Of all the different versions of tigers I've done, my favorite was on a young man from back East whose softball team used the tiger-head logo from what was then Esso/Humble oil (now ExxonMobile), with its famous slogan "Put A Tiger In Your Tank." Just like that tiger, the kid had a happy, infectious smile.

• A Leap of Leopards. I first met my friend Galen when I worked for the MUNI transit. After I started tattooing, he would periodically talk about his idea of doing a leopard on his arm. One day, while having drinks at the Lone Star Saloon, I suggested that, instead of a picture of a leopard, we do leopard spots — not as a single large piece, but rather as random areas of only a few spots.

This was inspired, in part, by humanoid aliens in the TV series "Star Trek: The Next Generation" and "Star Trek: Deep Space Nine," where at least one of the alien characters had random markings along the side of her face, not unlike light birthmarks. Also, it seemed to me that random areas of leopard spots would have a more organic quality, as though Galen had been born with them.

We both liked the idea, so at intervals across the space of about a year we would place spots. Some were on one of his feet extending a short way up his leg, some were to one side of his pubic area, some were on a shoulder, etc. After each session Galen would live with the work for a while, letting it "become" him. There were only a few of these areas, and the colors were subdued to seem more realistic.

At about the same time there was another TV series strikingly similar to "Star Trek NG" and "Star Trek DS9," but it was about a submarine crew instead of a space ship. I don't recall the title, and it didn't last very long, but I do remember that one of the "alien" humanoids was presented as amphibious, with a random pattern of spots similar to those on a frog.

I was intrigued by this use of random pattern and felt certain that tribal tattooing would morph enough to include more of it, but that proved to be an incorrect assumption.

• A Drove of Pigs. During the 1970s into the 1980s pig images and references were popular in the gay community, reflecting the seemingly insatiable sexual appetites of the "anything, anytime, anywhere" period, before the full impact of the AIDS epidemic forced people to reevaluate what they were doing. There was a gift shop in the Castro, the Obelisk, that stocked pig figurines, belt buckles, T-shirts, and tableware. While I was still tattooing at the Ambush, among my first tattoos was a pig's tail on a cute young guy with a great smile, who was quite successful at flaunting his new ink. Over the years I have drawn up leather pigs and biker pigs and even Miss Piggy wearing a harness and biker cap.

• A Den of Snakes. Among mankind's oldest mythological symbols, with a galaxy of different cultural and religious associations, snakes have consistently been a universal staple of tattoo iconography in both Western and Asian cultures. Their sinuous bodies, fascinating heads, and striking markings are immanently adaptable to tattoo art interpretations, either as stand-alone works or as part of a group of images.

Worldwide, the serpent is a powerful metaphor, associated with both negative and positive, or duality. Because it sheds its skin, it can represent rebirth or renewal . . . purification. It can represent sexual desire, while in other cultures it can be a guardian of sacred places. To some it represents fertility. It can also be associated with poisons and medicine.

Snake tattoos I've done have included: the Ouroboros — ancient symbol of a snake biting its own tail, with slightly different meanings in different cultures; the sixth sign of the Chinese zodiac; the Caduceus — the staff carried by Greek god Hermes, now the symbol of modern medicine; the Mayan Vision Serpent; and Kaa, the comical python in Disney's 1967 film version of Rudyard Kipling's *The Jungle Book*. The ancient Greek monster Medusa is included here because her hair was a mass of writhing, venomous snakes.

Other animals in the zoo collection have included a playpen of otters, one platypus, a gaze of raccoons, a small pack of wolves, an entire pod of various dolphins, killer whales, a pandemonium of parrots, a lounge of lizards, one large Komodo dragon (monitor lizard), a shiver of sharks, one squid, at least eight octopi, a few salmon (but not enough to constitute a run), a stare of owls, moray eels, and a city pound of pet dogs and cats. (For collective noun aficionados, I know that there is no known collective noun for panthers, who are solitary. Otters can be a romp, bevy, family, or raft, but I like the mental image of a playpen of otters).

Sometimes a client will ask if it's OK to bring a son or daughter to the appointment. I'm a big believer in parent-child bonding opportunities, so I always agree. Besides — I enjoy kids and enjoy showing them the tattoo process.

"Wanda" had brought along her daughter "Emily," who was about 6 or 7 years old. Mom had already explained the tattoo basics, and Emily excitedly plopped on a stool beside me. I showed her how the needle groups are put into the machines and let her step on the foot switch a few times. When I needed a dampened towel, she would dutifully spray it for me. After I bandaged Mom's new piece, I showed Emily a felt-tipped marker and offered to draw a small piece on her arm so that she, too, would have something to show off. Thinking she would choose a teddy bear or a favorite cartoon character, she quite surprised both of us when she firmly announced, "I want a shark!"

THE ETERNAL DRAGON

Natural events, the perils of the afterlife, the nature of disease, serendipitous good fortune, planetary motion, and our place in the heavens — all the mysteries of existence and even death itself are made easier to comprehend and deal with when embodied in the form of creatures we can't exactly see but believe are present. We may no longer outwardly believe in them, but our psyches do.

Modern tattooing and fantasy art are the great bastions of preservation of endangered imaginary species. Tattooers regularly dispense dragons, phoenixes, monsters, demons, and countless other critters.

In all of human history, spanning virtually all major cultures, there has been no archetypal symbol as powerful or as complex as the dragon. The dragon is a primal force, both destructive and creative. It is the volcano, the hurricane, the earthquake, and the tsunami. It is also wisdom and benevolence. It is fertility, life, existence, and growth. It can be cunning and cruel, or it can be valiant and noble and generous. It is a divine presence. For some, it is the universe itself.

It is also inclusive. A dragon doesn't care about your gender or if you're straight or gay or transsexual. A dragon looks directly into your soul and knows you for what you really are.

Very few other tattoo designs are as distinctive or make as commanding an individual statement as a dragon. Why people choose a dragon tattoo is as varied as the people themselves, but it doesn't take a psychology degree to figure out that one reason men get a dragon tattoo is to bolster their masculinity, to add a little boost of mental testosterone to their self-image.

When it comes to design dragon tattoos cover the stylistic gamut. There are Celtic dragons, tribal dragons, Asian dragons, Western Dragons. There are dragons from film such as Falcor, the dragon with dog-like features from the 1984 West German fantasy film *The NeverEnding Story* (*Die unendliche Geschichte*). There are cartoon dragons and dragons purloined from fantasy illustrations.

By habit, dragons are elusive creatures and trying to draw them is just as elusive, especially at first. Like most beginning tattooers I copied from existing flash designs. But even with all the models available the tattooer must spend a great deal of private time developing on paper in order to create a convincing dragon. Without attention to detail and a respect for the inherent drama, the result can end up looking like a bug squashed under glass.

Just like the dragon itself, a good dragon design is immensely fluid, conforming readily to body contours. And, as with the famous black panther design, it seems to move effortlessly with the body of the person who wears it. The body of the dragon can be patterned, it can have detailed scales, or even none at all. The single most important element, however, is the dragon's head. If the head is not convincing no amount of color or pattern or clever placement will convey the dragon's raw energy.

I tell clients that their tattoo should be "readable" from a distance of four to six feet away. A good tattoo should never be so small that it's unconvincing, and that's especially true for a dragon tattoo.

"Mark" came to the studio to get a piece on his forearm (as I recall it was to be God's finger touching Adam's finger, a detail from the famous Michelangelo fresco painting in the Sistine Chapel). A bodybuilder, Mark had an enviable physique and was clearly proud of his hard work at the gym.

On his left arm, in the middle of his 19-inch deltoid, was a coiled dragon no larger than the size of your index finger when folded completely down. It looked more like a larval dragon. It would have been better to have put it on a fish hook, attracting a large koi or maybe a trout, but I didn't dare to suggest that.

The Tattoo God's Universal Tattoo Truth #11:

When it comes to a tattoo, size does matter.

Sentimental Journeys

For more than a century a significant portion of tattoo parlor wall space has been set aside for designs dedicated to celebrating those persons who are important in our lives — compact testimonials of love and remembrance which seem strangely quaint in the company of all those other macho dragons, zombies, and fierce creatures clamoring for attention. For the peach-fuzzed young recruit in a foxhole in the middle of God-knows-where for God-knows-how-long, here was a surrogate touch of comfort from Mom or Lisa or Angie — a thin reflection of something hoped for and of an innocence lost forever.

For most gay men in the twilight of the 20th century there was no world war of marching armies, but there was a deadly enemy nonetheless. No matter the conditions it is a very human thing to invoke feelings of fondness, love, and caring, and to memorialize loved ones, grief, and pain.

It's unfortunate that a sentiment as lovely as a heart and flowers with "Mom" inscribed on the ribbon has come to represent, especially to non-tattooed people, the sum of all that's perceived as bad or wrong about tattooing. By some incomprehensible leap of non-logic, this poor little cliché is fuel for the cynical and jaded who yammer about the dire hazards of permanently marking one's body and who caution about the disease dangers to be found in the tattooer's lair. But at a time when crime is a constant rallying theme for politicians, U.S. prisons are filled to overflowing, and right-wing ultra-conservatives hate everybody, it seems to me that a healthy dose of sentiment and a few expressions of love could go a long way to make life a little nicer, a little easier.

Tattoos memorializing lovers, partners, and friends who succumbed to AIDS were steady reminders that life is all too brief. I still have the drawing for one of those, a simple flower and banner with the name "Bradley."

My favorite "Mom" tattoo was for a guy who wanted a really traditional mid-century style heart with flowers and classic cursive lettering for his mom's name. After giving it some thought for a day or so I called him and asked what were his favorite memories of her. He itemized a few, then happened to mention how he loved her apple pie. That caught my imagination, so we switched the heart for a slice of apple pie.

"Tyler" was a young man in his early 20s who came in for a tattoo of Elsie the Cow, the logo for the Borden Dairy Company in use since 1936. Elsie was his mom's favorite cartoon character, and he decided to place it on his upper leg.

Now Tyler was quite chatty, and we talked about a wide variety of topics. He also pointed out that his mom and I were similar in our views about the Vietnam War, politics, the hippie era, etc.

As it happened there was an antique toy truck displayed on one of the bookshelves, a real Buddy L "sand and gravel" dump truck manufactured during the early 1940s. It had been through its share of wear and tear and was a little beat up and a bit rusted. It had originally belonged to an uncle who passed away shortly before I was born, and I had inherited it.

When Tyler asked about it I told him that I had played with it when I was a kid and had kept it all this time. With wide eyes he looked at me, then back at the truck, then asked "Well just how old are you?" That really made me laugh. I looked at him and replied, "Believe it or not, kid, I'm older than Disneyland!"

THE THIRTIETH REASON

In his 1990 book, *Bad Boys And Tough Tattoos: A Social History of the Tattoo with Gangs, Sailors, and Street-Corner Punks 1950-1965*, gay professor, author, and tattooer Samuel M. Steward (aka Phil Sparrow) described being asked by his friend, famed sex researcher Alfred C. Kinsey, to compile a list of reasons why people choose to get tattooed. Sam dutifully came up with 29 reasons. Briefly, they are:

(Note: the topic titles are Steward's)

1. Decoration (of self)
2. Herd Instinct (part of the group)
3. Narcissism
4. Exhibitionism
5. Possession (of one person by another)
6. Sadomasochism
7. Rivalry (you got a tattoo, I'll get one too)
8. Homosexuality
9. Crypto-Homosexuality (male bonding)
10. Manhood Initiation Rite
11. Masculine Status
12. An Existential Act (the experience itself)
13. Compensation (to relieve feelings of inferiority)
14. Imitation
15. Compulsion (one tattoo isn't enough)
16. Celebration
17. "Aliveness" (just enjoying existence)
18. Non-Conformity and Rebellion

19. Gang Membership

20. Fetishism

21. Pastimes (nothing better to do)

22. Utilitarian (medical alerts, etc.)

23. Guilt/Punishment (all that "born to lose" stuff)

24. Advertisement

25. Sentimentality

26. Bravado, Braggadocio and "Wickedness"

27. Magic and Totemism

28. Religion, Consecration, Stigmata, and the Messiah Complex (whew!)

29. National and/or Ethnic Origins

Clearly, many of these motivations overlap, just as sexuality itself is difficult to categorize. There is, however, another motivation which Steward did not list, simply because he could not at the time have foreseen the events which came to shape it. The staggering impact of the AIDS epidemic brought about a tattoo impulse based on the sure and compelling knowledge that one's death is imminent. I call it the "Completion" motivation — tattoo as a pictorial talisman to help carry one into death and whatever might come after. This is remarkably similar to some tribal beliefs that non-tattooed persons are incomplete at death and may not derive after-life benefits.

The very first instance of this for me is indelibly burned into my memory. When he came into the studio, he appeared to be in his mid-twenties, quite thin, and it was obvious that he was very ill. He was shy, expecting to be turned away. He wanted a small phoenix on his chest, and when I asked him about it he told me that the phoenix represented rebirth and spiritual strength, and that if he could take this with him, the phoenix would help him make his transition. I did the piece, and he was gone within a month.

There is absolutely no preparation for something like this. I was staggered. I long ago forgot his name, but whenever I think about that amazing, sweet young man, I still get teary-eyed. I truly hope that he did, indeed, go to a better world.

There were a couple of other Completion tattoos that I recall. One of those was on a man in his mid-30s who wanted an angel flying upward at a diagonal angle across his entire back, looking skyward and with one arm raised. Just below the angel, going across his upper buttocks, was a stylized pond with lotuses and a dragonfly. We worked on it regularly over several sessions, but he passed away before we could complete all the coloring.

The Tattoo God's Universal Tattoo Truth #8:

No one ever promised that tattooing wouldn't make you cry sometimes.

1997 – 2000

By the mid-1990s those people diagnosed with AIDS were being prescribed a "cocktail" of combined drugs found to reduce the devastating effects of AIDS to a manageable state. With careful attention to medication times and doses, a person could add years to his outlook instead of only a few months. The daily regimen, however, required absolute adherence to a routine schedule with up to twenty or so pills at a time.

Tim was never diagnosed with AIDS. At each of his checkups his doctors determined that his viral load was sufficiently high, and he was not, therefore, a candidate for the cocktail. But I could see gradual changes taking place, and little by little he was becoming more fragile.

Because our bedroom was directly above my workstation we got a small device that generated white noise so that he could sleep a little better. There were settings that mimicked the sound of ocean waves, crickets, rain, etc. His favorite was "babbling brook," which sounded to me more like the gurgling of an aquarium pump. It could be heard downstairs, and frequently a client would ask, "What's that noise?" I would say, "What noise?" When they described the noise, I would say, "I don't hear anything. You're imagining things." Finally, though, I would relent and explain the sound.

The advent of personal computers and the phenomenal growth of the World Wide Web meant that even the rank and file could go online. Things like word processing, spreadsheets, databases, Web browsers, e-mail clients, and digital media were no longer the sole province of up-to-date businesses and computer geeks. As home personal computers became more affordable, even hillbilly Ma Kettle could go onto Netscape Navigator or Internet Explorer, find information, get news, and use e-mail to digitally communicate with anyone in the modern world. When Microsoft released Windows 95, the lines of people waiting to buy it extended down the street and around the block. Office supply stores offered all kinds of small computer applications. One of these that I got for Tim was a learn-to-type program designed as a computer game that was actually quite imaginative. In the movies, the ubiquitous "You've Got Mail" announcement of internet provider AOL became the title for a 1998 romantic comedy starring Tom Hanks and Meg Ryan.

The dot-com explosion was going full steam ahead. New internet companies were springing up at a dizzying, frantic pace, and it seemed as though any business name prefixed with "e-" or suffixed with ".com" virtually guaranteed heavy investment from venture capitalists. Coveted domain names such as business.com were being sold for millions of dollars.

I had resisted the personal-computer impulse, seeing nothing initially useful for the things we did. Standard mail, as far as I was concerned, worked just fine. Bound books on shelves held the information I needed. Neither of us had to do any writing to speak of. But then, I had also resisted answering machines until forced to use one for business.

Finally, we decided to take the PC plunge, and it wasn't

long before I became a fan, particularly of digital graphics.
One part of me wanted to move away from tattooing, and I
saw digital graphics as a way to do it. The whole computer
thing made sense to me, and I eagerly tackled graphics
applications in the same way I had tackled learning any
other art medium. But I would discover that this brave new
world was also ageist, even if by innuendo, and I had just
turned fifty.

Our ex-hippie landlady had been suffering from kidney
problems for some time, and she had been undergoing
dialysis treatments. She sold the Juniper Street property to
a developer and his business partner, both of whom lived
in San Mateo, a little past the San Francisco International
Airport. She passed away shortly thereafter. The new
landlord didn't like the idea of a tattoo establishment on
his property and tried at first to evict us, but he couldn't get
past the original zoning allowing artist live/work spaces.

I was growing a bit weary of tattoo conventions. The
last one I had attended was the April, 1996, National
Tattoo Association Convention in Tucson, AZ. Part of my
dissatisfaction was that the NTA conventions had become
rather predictable. It's true, though, that I also wasn't very
aggressive about getting in there, making myself known,
or setting up a booth, so I couldn't entirely blame NTA
organizers. Typically, a tattoo convention spans four
days, Thursday through Sunday. Thursday and Friday
are reserved for the professionals, and often include tattoo
contests for a variety of categories. Saturdays and Sundays
are open to the public, who can visit tattoo booths, peruse
artist portfolios, watch tattooing being done, buy books,

literature, and assorted T-shirts and knick-knacks.

Of all the conventions the very best was Tattoo Tour, formed in 1993 by tattooer Dennis Dwyer (Arizona) and J.D. Crowe (Virginia). Held at the Holiday Inn on Van Ness Avenue the event coincided with Fleet Week, a US Navy, Marine Corps, and Coast Guard extravaganza that includes deafening overhead demonstrations by the famed Blue Angels.

Tattoo Tour was the first to offer state-of-the-art seminars for professional tattooers seeking to further their education and were conducted by the top names in the business. Seminars I attended included two on machine building and repair, led by Lyle Tuttle. Dennis Dwyer led a seminar on current needle-soldering techniques. And for the first time the Alliance of Professional Tattooists conducted an extensive blood-borne pathogens class.

Van Ness Avenue is only a short block west of Polk Street. Before the Castro Street scene, Polk Street was a major gay enclave with numerous bars. It was known as the go-to place for most of the older, more genteel sweater set, as well as a known hangout for hustlers, many of whom were runaway teen kids.

Many tattooers print after-care instructions on the backside of their business cards. But after-care instructions can vary quite a bit from one tattooer to another. I had decided to collect as many business cards as possible just to compare instructions, so on Saturday morning I was going from one tattoo booth to another. It was fairly quiet as the doors for the public hadn't yet been opened.

As I neared a group of four or five guys I overheard their conversation. One was expounding on how he and his friend had gone over to Polk Street looking to get a beer somewhere and had wandered into — gasp! — a gay bar. As I eavesdropped he and his friend described how disgusted they were, how they felt like punching somebody's face, blah blah blah. I couldn't help myself. I interrupted, saying, "Well, guys, this *is* San Francisco. You walked into someone else's space and now you want to complain about it. All you had to do was walk back out. I suggest checking with the hotel information desk." The two grew hostile, but another of the group diffused the situation and they all moved on.

Even though gays and lesbians couldn't be legally married, there was progress toward greater equality in the workplace. More and more states were banning sexual orientation discrimination in the private sector, and numerous high-profile corporations were leading the way in recognizing domestic partnerships, extending health and other benefits to gay couples, and in decrying workplace discrimination.

On October 7, 1998, a young gay college student named Matthew Shepard was kidnapped, robbed, tortured, pistol-whipped about his head, and left tied to a fence just outside of Laramie, Wyoming. He died five days later, having never regained consciousness. When his death made national headlines Matthew Shepard became a symbol of anti-gay violence, renewing calls for Federal hate-crimes legislation. Predictably, far-right rhetoric about freedom of speech, reiterating their notions about the evils and rewards of the "gay lifestyle," abounded. Even in a city where we were already so accustomed to a steady onslaught of saddening obituaries, none were so jaded that they weren't deeply affected by the Shepard murder.

As we rolled into 1999 I decided that Mad Dog Tattoo needed a web presence, and I registered the domain name maddogtattoo.com. I had picked up a Microsoft application called FrontPage, a "what you see is what you get" (wysiwyg) application which promised easy theme-based website creation and administration without needing to know one whit about HTML coding. By any standard, that first website was awful, but Mad Dog Tattoo was now a part of the World Wide Web. Later on, for a variety of reasons, I would abandon wysiwyg editors altogether, preferring to hand code, which I found to be remarkably easy.

As the year 2000 approached there was worldwide apprehension and dire predictions of what would happen when 1999 ticked over to the year 2000. Referred to as the "Y2K Bug" or simply "Y2K," the biggest bugaboo revolved around concerns that, worldwide, computer programs using two-digit year values would cause problems when the year designation would suddenly become 00. This, in turn, would wreak havoc on everything: nuclear plant safety; bank systems; utilities providers; paper, food and fuel sources; domestic safety; the entire internet; global weather patterns; and online shopping. Doomsday prophecies abounded, predicting mass famines, the appearance of the Anti-Christ, the Battle of Armageddon, even the second coming of Jesus Christ. The Tattoo God had made no mention of any of this to me, but then he never gave me much notice about anything anyway. Incredibly, the world survived just fine.

In July, 2000, Vermont became the first state to legally recognize civil unions.

By the year 2000, the dot-com boom was fizzling. Companies that expected to strike it rich, like pets.com, failed miserably, and hundreds of millions of dollars of investment capital in assorted ventures vanished. During the boom property prices in San Francisco had risen sharply, as had rents. The gentrification of San Francisco was raising the financial bar all the way around. Many gays and lesbians, including a significant number of my tattoo clients, took advantage of the higher housing prices by selling their homes and then moving south to Palm Springs, where there was already a significant gay presence. Some people wanted a quieter, less hectic life. Cheaper housing and a lower cost of living appealed to those living with AIDS who were on disability or had a limited income. Some wanted to leave so much accumulated sadness behind. Others, of course, went elsewhere — places like the East Bay, small towns in the Sierras, or Oregon.

A HELPING HAND

Fisting, also called "handballing" or "fist-fucking," is the act of inserting a hand or even the entire forearm into someone's rectum.

While still in Arizona in the late 1970s I met a few guys at the old Club Baths in Phoenix who offered to introduce me to fisting, but I declined. The idea didn't appeal to me, and I have always personally believed the practice to be dangerous. But, to each his own.

By the time I had moved to San Francisco fisting was a regular practice, and its devotees sported a red bandana in the right or left hip pocket. At certain bathhouses and sex clubs there were special rooms equipped with leather slings and cans of Crisco® shortening for lubricant. There was a dedicated South of Market club called The Handball Express on Harrison, as well as the legendary Catacombs over in the Mission District on 21st Street between Guerrero and Valencia.

The image of a closed fist was the focal center for a variety of fisting-related tattoos, and on a few occasions I've tattooed a fisting measure on someone's arm, a kind of ruler indicating how far he will go in giving a friend a hand. These are placed along the inside of the forearm for easy visibility during fist-play.

The very first of these was during a trip to Amsterdam and was a fairly straightforward ruler going from the wrist to the inside of the elbow, measured in centimeters, and surrounded by biker-style flames.

Another one, brilliantly conceived by the client, was far more subtle. It was a simple series of chevrons (<<<<<), thin at the wrist but becoming thicker, wider, and farther apart as they progressed up his arm. Each chevron and each space between represented a unit of measure. To the casual observer, however, it was merely an interesting tribal design.

Now and then a client will appreciate my suggestions. I like those clients. This measure consisted of four cartoon animals, starting with a scared chicken at the wrist, followed by a plodding tortoise a little farther up the arm, then a hare in full sprint yet a bit farther on, and finally, just above the elbow, a pig eating an ear of corn.

Significant Others

There is an old saying that a camel is a horse designed by a committee. Every tattooer has had the experience of a client that brings along a partner, spouse, parent, or friend who is determined to chime in with their opinions about the tattoo — placement, colors, size, style, lettering — you name it, they've got an opinion about it. Even worse is when there are two or more people along for the ride, each suggesting something different. At times I've had to point out to them that the tattoo is the client's choice, not theirs, but some simply will not take the hint.

One of these was a "Dad" and his new "boy," a young man from Florida. I had done some work on the older man before and had found him to be annoyingly picky about all the details of his piece. The younger one had brought along some sketches of his concept for a large tribal back piece. He and I began working up a full-size layout, but more and more frequently, Daddy-o interrupted with his notions of how the work ought to look, and the result was predictably far different from what the younger one had in mind. Frustrated, the younger one finally said he would do the work some other time, and he eventually moved back to Florida — a wise decision.

A very young straight couple came to the studio. They were dressed simply, and it was clear that they were religious, especially the wife, who seemed a bit grim. She stated that "your body is a temple" and cited several Bible verses to prove that one's body shouldn't be marked or otherwise desecrated. He, however, was quite clear that he wanted this work and that his mind was made up even though she disapproved.

My immediate reply was, "Well, if your body is your temple, you should decorate it." I then went on to point out some facts: (1) the tattoo wouldn't change him, that he was still the same man she had fallen in love with, and (2) if he didn't do this, there was a good likelihood that he would become resentful down the road.

While we were doing the tattoo I continued to talk with her, making sure she was included in the conversation. Maybe she only needed to feel that she wasn't left out of the equation, or maybe she needed to know that he loved her. Whatever it was, she was in far better spirits when they left, and I hope that they were able to work things out.

I'm always happy to work with someone who comes in with his own artwork or a concept drawn up by a friend. Sometimes the drawing is easy to adapt, while sometimes a complete rework is necessary; but either way the result is unique to that person.

"Logan," who worked professionally as a graphic artist, came in with his own computer-generated design that he wanted put on his partner's butt cheek. He had printed it at the exact size he wanted it to be. It was a frontal view of a leaping tiger, complete with fangs, blue eyes, sharp claws — the usual stuff, including whiskers. Logan had his partner, who was a hefty guy, drop his pants so that I could see where this was to go.

The problem was that the entire tiger wasn't much larger

than the face of a wristwatch. When I tried to explain why his design was far too small, he got huffy about it. I then pointed out that there was plenty of room on that ass to put an entire family of tigers feeding on a zebra carcass. They both broke up laughing about that, and Logan relented.

A master/slave relationship is a definite commitment, and I have met both straight and gay couples who are as committed in their bond as any couple could be. For them it is far more than a bit of play S&M with a one-night stand — it's a way of life, and the love between them shines brightly.

"Stupid" came to the shop with his boyfriend, and I would guess them to have been in their mid-twenties. Stupid proceeded to tell me that he wanted me to tattoo his boyfriend with the word "SLAVE" in big letters across his chest, along with chains and "PROPERTY OF STUPID" lettering.

I turned to the boyfriend and asked if this was, indeed, what he wanted. After all, he was legally a free agent as far as I was concerned, and his consent mattered to me. He said that wasn't what he had in mind at all, that he actually wanted something "watery" on his upper left arm.

Stupid suddenly grew hostile, arrogantly demanding that the boyfriend obey, and that I take orders from Stupid and only from Stupid. I told Stupid that he was stupid. A row started between him and the boyfriend, so I demanded that they leave.

Some time later, at a Folsom Street Fair, the boyfriend ran up to greet me, telling me that he was no longer with

Stupid — that they had parted ways just after their visit to the studio.

One of the regular features of *Drummer* Magazine was a personals section titled "Tough Customers," and people from around the world placed ads, often accompanied by a photo.

One day I received a phone call from a guy who opened the conversation with "My master told me to call." He asked if I had seen one of the ads in which the Tough Customer photo was of the phrase "Fuck Hole" tattooed in the area between the person's scrotum and anus, along with an arrow pointing at his sphincter. I said that yes, I had seen it, so then the slave asked if I would be able to do that on him.

As it turns out, both he and his master were listening. My reply was, "Yes, I could certainly do something like that, but don't you find it rather redundant?" The master suddenly broke in to tell me what I could do to myself, then hung up.

While serving as a medic in the Army in 1970, I was stationed in Germany at the Landstuhl Regional Medical Center, the largest American hospital outside the United States. At the time, we were understaffed because of the Vietnam War, so the corpsmen frequently pulled duties that were outside their specific training.

One night I happened to be working in the Emergency Room when a group of guys were brought in who had gotten into a street fight with a German biker group. A few of the Germans were included, and we attended to them also. No one was too seriously hurt, and we dressed wounds, ordered X-rays for some, etc.

As a routine measure, we were required to administer tetanus shots. I was about to inject this big German thug who, only a couple of hours earlier, had wielded bike chains and been hit with fists and clubs when he, without any warning, fell to the floor in a dead faint at the sight of the syringe.

The Tattoo God's Universal Tattoo Truth #9:

The toughest-acting guys can be the worst wusses.

"Master Ryan," accompanied by his slave boy, wanted a classic black panther tattoo on his arm. As I worked on him he would flinch, hiss, make pained faces, and ask for frequent breaks. He was one of those self-identified tops who could dish it out but couldn't take it, and I felt a bit embarrassed for him, because his slave boy was sitting right there watching this unfold.

About a month later Master Ryan called to say he wanted to put the same panther on his slave boy's butt cheek, so we set the appointment. On the morning of the appointment he called to explain that the two of them had gotten into an S&M sex scene the night before, that there were a few cigar burns on the slave's butt cheek, then asked if that would be a problem.

I said that I couldn't know if there was a problem unless I could see what he was talking about, so I suggested coming in for the appointment anyway.

When the slave boy dropped his pants, both buttocks were covered with cigar burn scars and burns in various stages of healing. There was no space that hadn't been burned at some point. When I suggested putting the tattoo on a different spot, Master Ryan was insistent that it had to be where he wanted it. I then compared it to buying a brand new car only to enter it into a demolition derby, but there was no convincing the guy. I refused to do the piece.

The Tattoo God's Universal Tattoo Truth #10:

Look on the bright side: one minute of talking to a stupid client burns 17 calories.

ODDS AND ENDS

One of my tribal tattoo clients was a very handsome southern boy who not only modeled for some of the gay magazines but made many of his own outfits and gear for going out to clubs and bars. He believed absolutely that Preparation H® ointment, intended for hemorrhoid relief, was the best product for general skin care and for giving his tattoos that special glow. At the time the ointment, in a petrolatum base, had a yellowish color and smelled like fish oil. I have no idea what he must have smelled like on any given evening on the dance floor.

Through most of one Fall and into Winter I had worked on the image of a large Komodo dragon (monitor lizard), which extended from my client's right calf, up his right leg, and onto most of his back. He was a slender guy and had to be nude for several of those sessions.

Now San Francisco weather is cool to begin with, and rainy days can be downright cold. My studio was equipped with a small electric heater, and I had created an opening in the furnace duct which provided some additional heat when the upstairs thermostat kicked the furnace on, but the room could still be awfully chilly at times.

The tattoo process involves repeatedly wiping away excess ink with a paper towel dampened with soapy water, and even though I started out with hot tap water, it wouldn't take long before the water spray was pretty cold, and my client understandably hated that. Every time I sprayed him, he would shiver and sprout goose bumps.

One day he arrived with a gift of a small microwave oven, and thereafter I could warm the spray bottle at intervals, making him and other clients much happier.

One of the oddest tattoo projects to ever come through the door was of a line of ants traveling up the man's leg, across his abdomen, and onto his shoulder. I made the ants big, about 1-½ inches long. I tried mightily but without success to convince him that they should be going in and out of his ass, with some ants dragging an insect or picnic tidbits or maybe a candy.

Cigar aficionados are a dedicated fetish subset of the gay leather scene. There are social clubs, get-togethers, and cigar porn videos. One of these, "Sam," also had an enviable collection of vintage Disney memorabilia. The tattoo we came up with, a large scowling Donald Duck with a big fat cigar in his bill, amused me no end.

Now and then I have worked with a variety of modern pagans, wiccans, and Radical Faeries. I'm not familiar with all the finer distinctions, but runes, mystic symbols, and elements of indigenous spiritualities form the basis for many of their tattoos. A distinguishing feature is that, as a group, they have maintained the spiritual and inclusive ideas of the 1960s countercultural revolution.

"Donovan," a young gay man who lived in a Humboldt County (California) commune, brought along a handful of friends wearing hippie-style clothing and enough patchouli oil to render a rhinoceros comatose. They explained that the event was a ceremony and politely asked permission to be there. I had no problem with that, so I said, "sure."

The moment I started inking Donovan, the others suddenly began loudly wailing, chanting, and shaking a tambourine. I immediately stopped them and explained that my partner Tim, who worked extended overnight shifts as a psychiatric counselor, was sleeping in our bedroom directly above the studio. They looked truly stricken and disappointed, so in a spirit of compromise I asked, "Can't you just sit on the floor and hum?"

"Oscar" was one of those short guys who seem self-conscious of their physical stature and who compensate with their demeanor and gym-toned appearance. A Vietnam War veteran, every single one of his numerous tattoos related in some way to that period in his life. There were tributes to lost comrades, banners with his unit information, copies of his medals, classic patriotic pieces, images of weapons and helicopters, and a variety of slogans and dates.

What really struck me about this was that Oscar was one of those men who never got over it, who was never able to let it go. Sometimes other people's pain is almost touchable, and you can hardly bear to be around them for very long. Oscar was fortunate, though, in that he was able to maintain a job. So many Vietnam veterans in the City were homeless, standing on busy street corners with cardboard signs, who needed help but had been abandoned by the very people they had fought to protect.

One day I got a phone call from a guy who wanted a feather tattooed on the bottom of each of his feet because he had a tickle fetish. After explaining that the feathers would have to be small enough to fit within the middle of his arch because ink doesn't hold up well in calloused areas, he said that was fine, but that he had some concerns.

Caller: "I can't help it, but when I'm being tickled I involuntarily kick my feet."

Me: "Well, you have to hold still or I can't do the tattoo."

Caller: " Hmmm . . . maybe it would be a good idea to strap my feet down so I can't move 'em."

Me: "Hmmm . . . " (I could see where this was going)

Caller: "And I can't help it, but when I'm being tickled I laugh and yell."

Me: "Sorry, but you can't be noisy. Sudden shouts startle me and you wouldn't want a line to be messed up as a result."

Caller: "Well maybe if you used a ball gag . . ."

He then went on to ask if he could bring along a few friends for an evening appointment. We didn't do that tattoo.

A fire/water yin-yang symbol is a good example of graphically representing opposites and their relationship. Not only are the conceptual opposites handily juxtaposed, but it is also an exercise in using complementary colors. Another example would be Dorian Gray and his portrait.

But trying to combine opposites into one thing doesn't always work. The client came in with the idea of a single figure that would be both wise old man and innocent, unfettered youth. I don't know where he came up with the idea because he wasn't aware that each of these is a complicated archetype (a structural element of human psychology) explained at length by pioneering psychologist Carl Jung, who defined them by their Latin names *Senex* (wise old man) and *Puer* (eternal youth). They were explored even further by Jungian psychologist James Hillman.

In other words, there is no way that the two could be convincingly combined into a single figure, any more than one could combine fire and water into a single element. They could be juxtaposed like the yin and yang, but that's all. The more I tried to explain this, the more adamant the client became. Finally, he left.

"Jake" was a little bitty biker guy, about 5 feet 3 inches tall and so skinny you could clearly see his ribs. He wasn't ill, that's just how he was. Bravely, he wanted the entire Harley-Davidson logo on his chest — eagle, shield, banner — the works. Tattooing over bone can be downright uncomfortable for some people, and the sternum is one of the most painful places for tattoo work, especially over the xyphoid process — that little bone at the very tip of the sternum.

To his unending credit Jake was a real trooper about it, not complaining much. Somewhere into the second hour, though, he suddenly exclaimed, "Damn! All those feathers — and to think I could've settled for a T-shirt!"

Some people manage to put the "upid" in stupid, no matter what you tell them. "Mike" came in and got a tattoo on his ass cheek. As usual, I gave him his care instructions. He nodded and went on his way.

On that same evening he got stoned, went out, and ended up in some kind of kinky flogging scene. Two days later he called to say he had a problem, so I asked him to come in and show me. The tattoo was a hideous mess, and it was obviously developing a nasty infection. You gotta wonder who was more stupid, Mike or the guy doing the flogging. I told him to get his dumb ass to a doctor right away, and to be sure to tell the doctor what he had done so that I wouldn't be blamed for it.

"Robert" came in to get a piece on his abdomen and pubic area that had been designed for him by porn noir artist REX. He was a reasonably good-looking, fair-haired man, but was self-critical of his looks because he had no visible chest hair to speak of. It took some careful color mixing and a couple of hours to transform the appearance of his chest and give him a "treasure trail," and the result was actually reasonably convincing.

Some gay guys are turned on by large nipples and large aureolas. Nipple enlargement can include the use of snakebite kits, vacuum pumps, or simply stretching the nipple out and winding it with twine. Aureola enhancement is most often accomplished via tattooing.

One of the first guys to approach me about aureola enhancement wanted to expand them only slightly. It takes a bit of time to mix the right shade of reddish brown, but we succeeded. However, it wasn't very long until he wanted to expand them a wee bit more. Again, there was the color mixing issue. Predictably, he once more wanted an expansion. I told him this was a bit like adding tree rings. This time, and for every client thereafter who wanted aureola enhancement, I mixed up a fair-sized batch of color which I put in a 1-oz. plastic portion cup, pouring off only as much as needed for that session. I made the client take the cup of custom color home so that if he wanted the work expanded he could bring the color cup with him.

One day I got a phone call from a man claiming to be a scout for the "Jerry Springer Show." He explained that they were planning a TV segment on heavily tattooed teenagers, wanted to know if I had any tattooed teens as customers, and if so, asked if I was willing to give him their names or recommend them to him.

He listened politely as I explained at length that California law prohibits tattooing anyone under the age of 18, that I personally wouldn't tattoo minors for ethical reasons, and that I didn't know any tattooed teens or tattooers who worked on teens.

The whole thing gave me the creeps. The more I thought about that conversation, the more outlandish his story sounded. I concluded there were two possibilities: either he had some perverted interest in tattooed youngsters, which seemed pretty likely from his tone (see Universal Tattoo Truth #6), or he was an undercover law-enforcement agent trying to nab unethical tattooers or pedophiles. I'll never know.

"Vincent" was an amiable, middle-aged straight man who initially wanted a pair of simple, traditional-style pinup girls on his pubic area. Before long, he came back to get something else, and it was clear he had been bitten by the bod-mod bug because he was sporting a Prince Albert penis piercing and new nipple rings. While I worked on him he talked a lot about his growing fascination with body jewelry, tattoos, and extreme body modifications.

He began coming up with his own geometric tattoo designs. When the tattoo had healed, he would then go to a body modification practitioner in Arizona who placed subdermal implants underneath selected portions of the tattoo so that those portions created a raised design. He continued to add piercings and enlarge piercings he already had in place. I had met his wife, a pleasant person who worked at an office not far from the studio, but I made it a point never to discuss Vincent's tattoos or modifications.

Vincent reached a point where he seemed to always have something healing whenever he came to the studio. There were two very large, finger-thick rings through his entire scrotum, and I wouldn't even try to guess the combined weight of all the rings and barbells in his penis. I would tease him that I could tell by the sound whenever he entered the alley from Folsom Street.

Doing that much modification at a time meant that there was some rejection, and he told me of a couple of episodes that required him to see a physician because of infections. A few other times he had to have a subdermal implant removed because it had shifted or become infected or both, but he always replaced it later on.

Vincent then had his penis enlarged with silicone, resulting in a permanent erection. I'm not certain if that was accomplished by injection or insertion of silicone rods. I have no idea why he felt he needed this, as his penis was certainly above average in both length and girth.

I hadn't seen Vincent in a year or so when one day he called to say that he needed the original pinup girls repaired. When he arrived for his appointment, I was astonished to observe that he no longer had a penis. Instead, he now had a vagina, and what remained of his penis formed a large clitoris. There was a surgery scar crossing the pinup girls, and that was why he came in for the repair.

He explained that the silicone had begun to migrate backward into his body and that he had waited too long before seeking professional help. His surgeon told him that the silicone had advanced so far into his body that the only recourse was surgery that would necessarily include removing his penis entirely.

When Vincent asked the doctor about creating a vagina, he was told that he would be required to gender-identify as a female and begin hormone treatments before any such surgery could take place. Not willing to identify as a female, Vincent had the surgery done in Thailand.

A few months later I ran into Vincent and his wife at an event. Vincent had gotten modest breast implants and his eyebrows were now small tribal tattoos; and he was wearing a regular men's suit and tie. Over the years I have consistently marveled at Vincent's special brand of courage to just be himself, take things as they come, and reinvent himself.

2001 – 2007

To those who had spent any amount of time there, it came as no surprise when The Netherlands became the world's first nation to legalize same-sex marriage in April, 2001. My own experiences in Amsterdam had shown the Dutch to be very accepting of queer folk. I'm sure that there was probably a religious element that disapproved of gay marriage, but they were not enough of a deterrent to such sweeping reform.

Tim's health was continuing to decline incrementally, and he was subject more and more to inexplicable opportunistic infections and diseases. At one point he experienced a very serious attack of Hepatitis B, requiring immediate hospitalization. His skin and eyes had taken on the telltale yellow tint, and his body was painfully swollen with retained fluids. One doctor, spying all his tattoos, immediately put the blame there. His viewpoint was one shared by a surprisingly large number in the medical profession who still believe that tattooers are ignorant of standard procedures regarding blood-borne pathogens. I was incensed at such a blanket statement and pointed out that I was always hyper-careful about safe practices and mentioned the Alliance of Professional Tattooists (APT). But it fell on deaf ears. Because Tim worked at a ten-day residence alternative to psychiatric hospitalization, we figured that he must have contracted hepatitis there.

Worry about Tim's condition caused me to make one of the most glaring tattoo mistakes of my entire career. Every tattooer makes an occasional mistake, but most of the time it can be corrected on the spot, and the client never even knows it. But not this one. The tattoo was of an angel holding out something like a crystal ball. I had failed to make the crystal ball a perfect circle, and it was noticeably flat along one side. I think there might have been something else as well. Having spotted it, the angry client returned to the studio the following day to show me. To make matters worse, he wasn't about to let me try to remedy things. I felt deeply embarrassed, and refunded all his money.

The Tattoo God's Univeral Tattoo Truth #12:

Shit happens. Deal with it honestly, move on, and don't let the shit define you.

Our diet had always included fish and shellfish. But then Tim mysteriously developed an intense allergy to shellfish. His first allergic episode we chalked off to possible food poisoning. His second episode, however, was frightening, causing his face and tongue to discolor and swell, and restricting his breathing. It didn't take long for the reaction to extend to any kind of fish. His doctors were as mystified as we were.

On Tuesday, September 11, 2001, the country and the world became riveted to the news that two hijacked airliners had been flown directly into the North and South towers of New York's World Trade Center, another had been crashed into the Pentagon, and that yet another had failed in its mission to target Washington, D.C., when passengers attempted to overcome the hijackers.

The story unfolded for weeks. Speculation mixed with known facts dominated all news reports and finally became so unrelenting that we stopped watching the news for a while. In 2002, we learned of the creation of the Department of Homeland Security, we learned about the USA Patriot Act, and that the National Security Agency (NSA) had been granted extended powers. Air travel became a checkpoint nightmare for thousands of people. We watched the comedy of excuses and posturing at the United Nations leading up to going to war with Iraq in 2003. And we watched sadly as many Americans turned on their Middle-Eastern neighbors.

One of our favorite television sitcoms was "Will and Grace," about a gay lawyer (Will Truman) who shares a New York apartment with his female best friend and ex-fiancé (Grace Adler). Their friends Jack McFarland, also gay, and wealthy alcoholic socialite Karen Walker rounded out the cast. The first thing that made the show remarkable was that there were gay characters and that the characters were both believable and believably human. The show was subtly made acceptable to most of America in that, like most couples' sitcoms, it revolved around the relationship between a man and a woman, even though the leading man happened to be gay. Thirdly, the Will Truman character was that of a romantic guy searching for Mr. Right instead of playing the field and bringing home tricks. Occasionally there was included a gay couple, Joe and Larry, who were obviously committed to their relationship and who had adopted a daughter. Popular culture shapes people's views on political issues, and "Will and Grace" was actually a formidable force in helping people be more accepting. Seven years after the series closed in 2006, failed Republican presidential hopeful Rick Santorum would bitterly blame "Will and Grace" for growing acceptance of nationwide gay marriage.

In May, 2004, Massachusetts became the first state to legalize gay marriage. A few months later one of my tattoo clients told me he was leaving San Francisco to move to Massachusetts so that he could get married and adopt. I'm not certain if he already had a partner, but his complete sincerity in wanting to be a parent deeply impressed me.

My interest began to turn back to oil painting. I hadn't done any painting for quite some time, always busy with tattoo art or tinkering with digital art. But there's something soothing about putting paint onto canvas, in the same way that the simple act of kneading bread can be calming. And I was renewing my interest in the human figure. This time, though, I wanted my work to be something more than typical erotica, and I began exploring larger themes that still utilized the male form.

Each October, ArtSpan, a nonprofit organization, organizes SF Open Studios, showcasing hundreds of emerging and established artists in their studios. There is also the SF Open Studios Exhibition, where each participating artist hangs one work, and the Exhibition is open through the entire month. Each weekend focuses on a different section of the city and, using a printed guide, collectors and admirers can walk from one studio to another. My first Open Studio featured only a few pieces, but I actually did well and felt encouraged to keep doing more.

One day Tim fell and broke his arm while coming up our steps. At the hospital he had to endure having the broken bone realigned in a process called "reduction," then put in a sling for a few days until any subsequent swelling subsided. His doctors debated whether to put his arm in a cast or do fixation device surgery involving plates, nails, or screws. They decided on a cast. His arm never completely healed, and his use of it remained limited. There would be X-rays and then a wait-and-see period, then more X-rays and more wait-and-see. On work days he would strap on a plastic sleeve-sling, which meant that he had trouble driving our beat-up Mitsubishi hatchback with its manual transmission and lack of power steering. I wanted to trade the car in for something easier to drive, but he was adamant.

Watching someone you love slowly die has to be one of the most painful, heartbreaking experiences you can ever have. We both knew what was coming and were afraid to try talking about it. What was there to say? Each of us already knew that the other wanted simple cremation, with no memorial services, epitaphs, or obituaries. What we did do was take time each day to hold each other and tell each other of our love. Differences that at one time seemed important were now in the distant past and no longer had any relevance whatever. We made little jokes. We smoked cigarettes on the landing in the wee hours of the morning, listening to the two foghorns, "Booper" and "Beeper," croon to each other. We marveled at each new bloom on our orchid wall. We practically memorized T.S. Eliot's *Four Quartets*. We talked about our landlord, who had never done anything except what was absolutely required to maintain the cottage. And we got through each day.

A four-story gray box of condos went up in the vacant lot next to us. It completely blocked our bathroom window and butted literally right up against the wall of the cottage and the front building. The once-sunny courtyard was now in shade for most of the day. The new neighbors complained about any smoke or odors coming from my charcoal grill. They hated that homeless people came down the alley to relieve themselves, and supported an effort to fine someone almost a hundred dollars for doing what any dog, including their own, was allowed to do.

I began encouraging Tim to write a will. He resisted. I showed him how easy it was to create a will online. We already had durable powers of attorney in place. He continued to put it off, even after I created my own will and gave him a copy.

Then, mysteriously, Tim lost his voice. He speech was reduced to a hoarse whisper. Once again, his little team of doctors had no explanation, no treatment. He continued working, though, and his coworkers, friends whom he had known for years, pampered him on his shifts. We would joke about his voice because he sounded like some kind of 1940s film noir mob thug, especially over the phone. He stopped doing night shifts. He had always done our laundry at work, but I began taking it to a nearby laundromat so that he wouldn't have to be lugging the bags.

I continued to nag him about making a will, threatening him that if he didn't do this I would track him down in the afterlife and break his other arm. He finally relented when I pointed out that his dad and sister could come in and decide not only about cremation, but that they could try to legally claim virtually anything in the house, because there was no way to distinguish who had owned what.

I began limiting my own work so that I could spend more time caring for him. We spent our evenings watching television or movies we rented from Netflix. He had grown uncomfortable sleeping in the bed, so he began sleeping upright in the living room, in one of a pair of modern-design reclining chairs. I provided him with a broom handle that he could use to tap on the wall or floor if he needed anything.

Once more he went back to the hospital, this time for what turned out to be some kind of fluid buildup around his heart. A new cardiac oncologist was added to the team, and when a biopsy of the fluid came back benign, she told us that she had never before seen such a case like that because she fully expected a malignant something or other. She quickly became Tim's favorite doctor, partly because of her total honesty with us. This time, though, Tim did not return to work. His deterioration was like watching a time lapse video of a wilting flower.

Then came the bad news day. His favorite doctor sat us down and said there was nothing more that they or anybody could do. She gave us a list of hospice services, but I had already promised Tim that I would never take him to one. She prescribed some extra medications for "discomfort," arranged for an oxygen setup to be delivered, and I took him home. The oxygen was delivered the next day, but it was rather pointless. His mind was already drifting, and he slept — if you could call it that, most of the time. I sat next to him in our chairs and listened to his breathing change and become more ragged.

Finally, at around three in the morning on February 6, he was gone. I sat in the quiet for almost an hour. Even

Booper and Beeper seemed subdued. The police were the first to be called. An ambulance arrived as part of standard procedure, and then the medical examiner arrived. I had to haul out Tim's will. The medical examiner asked if I had a crematory in mind, and when I said no, he did something rather surprising by asking me to bring him a Yellow Pages. Explaining that he wasn't allowed to recommend one service over another, he showed me the listings under "Cremation," but kept noticeably putting his finger on one in particular. I took the hint. After a lot of official stuff I was instructed to wait in the street while they wrapped him because rigor mortis had already set in, and they didn't want me to witness what they had to do. By the time everyone was finally gone daybreak was well underway. I called Tim's workplace and then I called Tim's dad.

Tim was never diagnosed with AIDS. The official cause of death was small-cell carcinoma — lung cancer. At no previous time was lung cancer ever discussed as a possibility.

I managed to stay on Juniper Street, but the nine hundred dollar a month rent was a lot for one person to manage. Locked into rent control, the landlord wasn't about to initiate any property improvements. Within a year I had decided to leave San Francisco. I considered a few options, but on a visit to Palm Springs I connected with a high-end gallery in Palm Desert, was offered work at Anarchy & Ink Tattoo, a walk-in tattoo shop in nearby Cathedral City, and became aware of the very active desert gay community. With both a gallery and a job waiting for me I closed up shop, said

goodbye to San Francisco, and left for Palm Springs in June,
2007.

Epilogue

Tim's passing coincided with an already passing era in gay history. Gay culture is being assimilated into a larger social context, and gay culture is being redefined. This may or may not be good, depending on how one looks at it. Author James Baldwin pointed out that one of the hazards of demanding, and achieving, acceptance is that the very acceptance we demand comes with a price tag — acceptance is on the terms of the larger social culture.

To some that's a bad thing. But many of the people who think so live in a wistful, myopic reverie where macho gay men should still be under the social radar, or that they should at least want to be. But the gay scene and the gay leather scene simply cannot remain stuck in a time warp. Thankfully, the scene is evolving before our very eyes. Younger men and women worldwide are defining the world in their terms, not ours. That doesn't mean they don't appreciate those of us who worked so hard to get things to where they are now. They do. Nonetheless, it is they who are defining what's relevant for today and for the tomorrows to come.

I love watching where things are going. While the formalities of the old-school leather kink scene are actually remarkably intact, gay culture now has Goths and Emos and Furries who are shaking things up and bringing fresh ideas.

In the U.S., same-sex marriage equality is finally a reality. There is a new and wider horizon for transgender acceptance. Now there are gay homecoming royalty, transgender beauty queens, and same-sex military marriages; and adoptive gay couples are portrayed in starring roles on primetime television.

There are still brutal anti-gay hate crimes. There are still powerful religious bigots. There are still nations who marginalize and even execute homosexuals. But the tide is turning, and the tide is turning more rapidly than ever before. Personally, I'm convinced that handheld communication, instant messaging, and the apps phenomenon are what will change the world as people learn that they're really not so different from each other.

All of this is already having an effect on gay tattooing. Just as tattooing itself is embracing street art influences, manga drawing, Japanese animé art, and steampunk, gay-specific art is exploring those same elements. With the advent of gay assimilation into American mainstream society there is also less of a perceived need for the defiance in gay tattooing that was so prevalent earlier.

I'm considered a tattoo old-timer now, and, like any old-timer, I'm opinionated about a lot of things. But even an opinionated old fart can't help but marvel at what's coming up. That old Tattoo God isn't just sitting back in his Hawaiian shorts, sipping mojitos, and singing raunchy songs. He's a busy guy. I think his name is Mike.

If you've made it this far, thank you for reading.

Robert E. Roberts, aka mad dog.

Appendix A: The Tattoo God's Universal Tattoo Truths

The Tattoo God's Universal Tattoo Truth #1:
Inevitably, "Property Of" tattoos and names of boyfriends or girlfriends are a jinx, and a breakup will likely be only a matter of time.

The Tattoo God's Universal Tattoo Truth #2:
Tattoo clients hear care instructions in a foreign language.

The Tattoo God's Universal Tattoo Truth #3:
Your tattoo designs, no matter how simple, are worth money. Hang onto them.

The Tattoo God's Universal Tattoo Truth #4:
No matter how carefully you measure for an armband, when you go to put on the transfer there will be either an overlap or a gap.

The Tattoo God's Universal Tattoo Truth #5:
No tattoo will make you more masculine than you already are, no amount of tattooing will make you look like that person in the magazine photo, and pink is only a color. Get over it.

The Tattoo God's Universal Tattoo Truth #6:
When you least expect it, somebody's getting off.

The Tattoo God's Universal Tattoo Truth #7:
There is always someone with a tattoo idea you never imagined.

The Tattoo God's Universal Tattoo Truth #8:
No one ever promised that tattooing wouldn't make you cry sometimes.

The Tattoo God's Universal Tattoo Truth #9:
The toughest-acting guys can be the worst wusses.

The Tattoo God's Universal Tattoo Truth #10:
Look on the bright side: one minute of talking to a stupid client burns 17 calories.

The Tattoo God's Universal Tattoo Truth #11:
When it comes to a tattoo, size does matter.

The Tattoo God's Univeral Tattoo Truth #12:
Shit happens. Deal with it honestly, move on, and don't let the shit define you.

INDEX

A

B

CPSIA information can be obtained
at www.ICGtesting.com
Printed in the USA
BVHW04s1443240518
517257BV00001B/56/P